MW00655291

HOME EARLY

Destroy Distraction,
Become Powerfully Productive, And
Finish Work Before Dinner

HOME
EARLY

MICHAEL J. MEHLBERG

Copyright © 2020 by Michael J. Mehlberg
All rights reserved.
ISBN: 978-1-7349893-0-4

To anyone who struggles...
To anyone who feels overwhelmed...
To anyone who has lost their balance, their discipline, their control...

...and is willing and ready to take it back.

Download the Worksheets and Bonuses Free

Thank you for buying Home Early. Grab the free worksheets and other bonuses (listed below) at www.michaelmehlberg.com/homeearly.

- **Time Pie Worksheet** to help you find a few hours of free time in your day.

- **Purpose Exercises** to help you find direction and purpose in all seven areas of your life.

- **9 Purpose Questions** to help you discover your North Star, your reason for being.

- **Habit Tracker** to help you visualize and solidify positive habits every single day of the year.

- **Mind, Spirit, Body Checklist** to help you keep all aspects of yourself and your environment firing on all cylinders.

Note: The stories in this book are true, told only from my perspective. Anyone named herein refers to a real person though their identity has been obscured to protect their privacy.

Acknowledgments

To Aaron, my brother, for his insight, his support, and his unending interest in my progress and frustrations with this book. He kept me writing. He kept me positive. These pages are in print because of him.

To Marcus and Jen Brodfuehrer, my neighbors and friends, for their practical ideas, feedback on extra-shitty early drafts, and the motivation to keep on writing for someone other than myself.

To Kacie Main, my content editor, for believing in my ideas and system for getting things done, even when my writing wasn't telling the right story or telling the story right. She helped me see who this book could help and gently guided me to the right words and lessons.

To My children, for teaching me what really matters in a world of constant distraction, never-ending projects, and one-upmanship. They have given me more than I could ever give to them, and I'm prouder of them than of anything else I've ever done.

And most of all, to Elaine, my wife, for her constant support and unwavering belief that this book could be more than I ever thought possible. She elevated my game. She raised the expectations I had for myself. I'm a better writer for it, and everyone reading this book is better off because of her.

Table of Contents

HOME EARLY

Introduction

Racing Rats

"You wonder if it is truly possible to enjoy a life where you can 'Play Longer.' You wonder if the rat race our society seems to be in is all that there is, and would love to find another way to enjoy life with your family and friends."

— Tara Ross, Work Smarter, Play Longer

In the Midwest, it was hard to find good software engineers in the late '90s. But my Lead Engineer was a fucking rock star. She had an outstanding year, produced incredible results, and was about to sit down to a glowing performance review, delivered by yours truly. But the look on her face told me something was very, very wrong. No sooner had I thanked her for her dedication to our team and company did she collapse, head in hands, with tears streaming down her cheeks. The time we'd set aside to review her performance quickly turned into a conversation about balancing work with her personal life—including her pending divorce.

Three thousand miles west, a hugely successful loan officer in San Francisco found himself frazzled and burnt out at the end of each day. He could never seem to get enough done, pushing himself to the limit but never finding the end of his task list. His mind was, as he said, "all over the place." He'd jump from one task to the next without finishing either. Though he'd read every article on productivity, every book on getting things done, and every life-hack known to man, no tool, tip, or tactic could solve his overwhelm. So, after years of struggle and with no other ideas, he used his financial success to install a bathroom in his office. It was a final attempt to save a few minutes every day. A last-ditch effort to catch up. But it didn't help. A month later, he felt more stressed than before; his last strands of sanity and control flushed down the toilet, now literally less than 10 feet away.

Back home in Virginia, my own son sat fretting over a simple choice: a.) do his math homework now and play video games later or b.) play with friends now and do his homework later. His inability to make a decision transformed into deep frustration, building so much that he cried and snotted all over the table. He pulled his hair in despair over how many math problems there were. He whined about how he'd have to "show his work". His sense of overwhelm was so profound, he rode an emotional roller-coaster for an hour before giving up. In the end, he didn't get his homework done, couldn't play with his friends, and wasn't allowed to play video games. It was the worst of all worlds.

These are the stories and struggles of real people whose circumstances may have been unique but who faced the same struggles we all do. Struggles that stem from the same sense of overwhelm, disorganization, and chaos. None of which are our fault.

Like them, you and I have a sense for how our lives should look. We have a vision for how we want to live. We may even have goals to support that vision. But nobody taught us how to realize it. Nobody taught us how to set goals, break them down, track them to completion, and actually achieve them. There was no class in high school on living a productive, successful, and balanced life. And so, we do the best we can. We follow our instincts, which ultimately, is letting luck and circumstance guide our days.

I know. It doesn't seem fair. After all, it's not like we need to live lavishly. We know we don't *need* a life full of excess. We're just looking for a happy, mostly untroubled life of accomplishment, meaning, and peace. Success doesn't mean billions in the bank. It means a life of balance. And I'm here to tell you that despite what our culture pressures us to do, we can't hustle and grind our way to this kind of success. Science proves it.

PART I

The Myths and Truths of Productivity

The rats' race and the stress distresses until we start down a new path

"It is not that we have a short time to live, but that we waste a lot of it." — Seneca

^ Translation: Life is short if you waste it.

Chapter One

Stressed and Distressed

"This is progress in America. You always move forward and there are
no limits to how far you can go or how fast you can get there. Don't
pause, don't reflect. You win or lose. You'll fall behind and fail if you
stop moving. Fast at any cost is the mantra of a stressed and
distressed American society today."

– Dr. Stephanie Brown, Society's Self-Destructive Addition to Faster
Living, New York Post

Living a balanced life implies being calm, in control, and stable. But
it's hard to be any of these things when we're constantly on the
move, striving to live up to the standards defined by our "hustle
culture."

We're pushed to do more and be more. Land another promotion.
Earn another degree. Increase our income, grow our circle of friends,
give our kids a pain-free childhood, maximize our influence on
important social issues. For fuck's sake! It's why thousands of business

mentors and life coaches line the streets, throwing productivity tools our way so we can get more done in less time with less money. They stand ready to capitalize on this way of life, promising to take us to that next level of relationship, career, and financial success. We're rewarded for driving ourselves to the limit, for never stopping, for never relenting, for living big and fast and perfect. It's why we see the pace of life increasing before our eyes.

In a 2007 study commissioned by the British Council, researchers found that urban populations walk 10% faster than they did in 1990 and upwards of 30% faster in monster cities like Singapore. While it may seem counterintuitive, walking faster, the very act of which increases your heart rate and strengthens your heart muscle, is correlated with heart disease ("What walking speeds say about us," 2007).

People are walking faster to get more done, and in trying to get more done, they are not eating as well, exercising less, and not socializing with friends and family. It's leading them to be stressed and distressed. And, while faster-paced cities like Singapore have higher happiness levels and an overall feeling of well-being, this is mainly due to cultural factors such as social support, reduced corruption in business and government, and generosity ("Singapore ranked 2nd-happiest," 2019). In many countries (including America) where we barely take time for lunch and treat charity as a business strategy, the speed of life becomes unbalanced such that we succumb to stress-related diseases and psychological overload. Because of this, the benefits of a brisk walk (which include an improvement in heart and lung function, reduced risk of stroke and diabetes, decreased weight, and even reduced risk of depression) are outweighed by the adverse effects of relentless stress.

Technology is the suggested culprit: "We're just moving faster and faster and getting back to people as quickly as we can - and that's minutes and not hours. That's driving us to think everything has to happen now," said Professor Richard Wiseman, head of this study. This is problematic because when everything has to happen now, making progress on important, longer-term goals feels impossible.

#

One moment, you're working on a project. The next, a phone call comes in. You get distracted and read an email. Then, forgetting what you were initially working on, you start a completely different task. Someone stops by your office to chat until you end up at lunch—a lunch you're likely working through. Your afternoon is riddled with meetings, which are interwoven with more interruptions. Every time you sit down to work on something of value, an urgent email comes in, the phone rings, a meeting reminder chimes, or there's a knock on your door. And, that's not even accounting for personal distractions.

Social media, text messages, and breaking news demand your attention with clickbait headlines too enticing to pass up. By the end of the day, you're exhausted from nonstop interruptions and continual effort, but feel as though you haven't accomplished anything. For all the running around, you have nothing to show for the things that matter—important work projects, family, hobbies, side-hustles. They've all atrophied from lack of attention.

It's enough to make you scour the Internet for life-hacks; tricks to optimize your time and expand your energy. In the search for destroying distractions and becoming a productivity monster, I did. Each hack seemed to contain some bit of wisdom, either because it was a novel concept or because it was used by the rich and famous. We are attracted to the idea of massive success and are eager to try anything or follow anyone in order to find the time and money to do what we want. Thus, if Elon Musk advocates meditation, our desire to be a self-made millionaire compels us to tangle our legs into lotus position for an hour every morning. If Dwayne Johnson wakes up at 3 a.m. to crush weights for four hours, we feel momentarily motivated to do the same. Each life-hack presented to us is like a glittering morsel of potential that, once consumed, holds the promise of a life of achievement and happiness.

But for every successful person who meditates, there's one who doesn't. And, for every Instagram celebrity waking up at the ass crack of dawn, there's one who stays up late and sleeps in. This makes each hack less of a solution and more of a shiny lure, sparkling in a dreary ocean of grit and hard work. Unfortunately, like a lure, if we bite, we find ourselves getting dragged around, wasting time trying to make yet another productivity tactic work for us.

The problem is, while waking up early, meditating, or working out can all be important aspects to an overall system, blindly biting hook, line, and sinker into every life-hack without considering the ramifications can result in, at best, minor improvements and, at worst, a massive distraction to your goals. It's why every success tactic you've found leaves you right back where you started: working late, exhausted, and wondering what happened to your day.

The fact of the matter is, these life-hacks may have worked for someone at one time in their life. But most successful people have already been grinding, climbing, and putting in a tremendous amount of effort to get where they were going. The life-hack may have taken them to the summit, but it didn't help them scale the first 99% of the mountain.

Life-hacks aren't the answer then. They are optimizations to a system that's already working. They are the tiny aerodynamic adjustments to a space shuttle that's already built and ready for orbit. With the right productivity system in place, a good life-hack will further refine that system, making you more productive as a whole. Without that system, every life-hack is a distraction from your goals and a temporary avoidance to a long-term productivity problem.

#

It's easy to think of productivity as some guy sipping coffee, phone at his ear, balancing a computer in his lap while reading the news on his commute to work. You know, the ultimate multitasker. Maybe you know someone like this. They're that friend who can never hang out because they're working late. Or the few times you do see them outside the office they're buried in an email on their phone. Or, maybe *you* are this person? You've trained yourself to triage emails while on a conference call over dinner (been there). In search of that elusive feeling of accomplishment, you try to maximize every moment of your day with multitasking efficiency, only to find yourself exhausted and with nothing to show for your efforts.

That's because productivity isn't about burning the candle at both ends. Productivity, rather, is about burning the candle just bright enough, just hot enough, that you light everything around you while still having more candle to burn tomorrow. It's about sustained output on essential tasks. Tasks that matter. Tasks that make a positive difference in your life. Tasks that help you make more money, get stronger, be healthier, reduce stress, and (excuse the cliché) live your best life. Productivity is about managing your time effectively to get the important things done without losing sight of other aspects of your life, becoming unbalanced, or sacrificing your humanity for someone else's end goal.

If you can make real progress on a goal to achieve a personal dream while maintaining balance at work, you can call yourself productive. If you can take a step forward toward the vision you have for your life while keeping a thriving family, you can call yourself productive. If you can complete an important milestone in your business while staying healthy, you call yourself productive. Because those uniquely human experiences—enjoying dinner with your family, relaxing with a hobby, or enjoying a night out with your friends—don't reduce your productivity. They enhance it.

None of this happens using life-hacks. But it doesn't happen by accident either. Productivity happens with a disciplined approach to goal setting and planning. It happens by following a system. Unlike a life-hack that might work once, the right productivity system will *continually* increase the amount of work you can get done on any given day. Unlike a happy accident, the right productivity system will help you *consistently* produce results. And, unlike the hustle-and-grind culture that demands we do more with less, the right productivity system will help you get important work done, feel accomplished, and still make it home for dinner.

We're here to build that system for you now. We'll design it around *your* life's purpose and focus it on creating and tracking and managing goals that allow *you* to live your life's vision.

What this system won't include are hacks for relentlessly multitasking like the guy described above. Nor will it include strategies for mindlessly jamming more shit into your day. These ideas of productivity are myths that hold us back. Unfortunately, they aren't the only ones.

Chapter Two

The Myths of Productivity

*"Once you have mastered time, you will understand how true it is
that most people overestimate what they can accomplish in a year –
and underestimate what they can achieve in a decade!"*

— Tony Robbins

If I asked you which country was the most productive in the world,
what would you say? Japan? America? Those were my answers, but
they're not even in the top five.

Every year, Expert Markets studies the productivity of countries
around the globe. Their measurement stick isn't hours worked per
week. Instead, they calculate average hours worked divided into the
income generated toward the country's gross domestic product
(GDP). In other words, how much dough the average citizen earns per
hour of effort. What they found flies in the face of the conventional
wisdom.

Myth #1 — Work More, Be More Productive

Though money isn't the only measure of success, when measuring productivity output across an entire country, tracking money earned per hour worked makes sense. The Expert Markets study found that the countries that work the most per week actually earned the least.

For example, while the average American worked 33.9 hours per week and earned $65.43 GDP per hour worked in 2018, Luxembourg citizens worked, on average, five hours less per week and earned $83.93 more ("How Luxembourg Rose," 2017)! Luxembourg isn't the only example. Norway workers hustled 6.5 hours less and earned $24.37 more. Ireland workers worked 1.1 hours less and earned $22.88 more (Bradshaw, n.d.). The list goes on. And, while there are some outliers, the trend stays consistent: The more hours worked, the less money earned. The fewer hours worked, the more money earned.

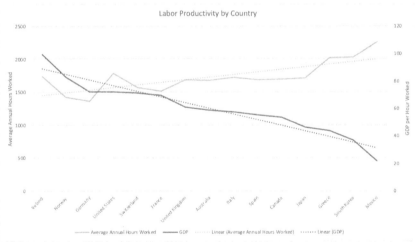

Data sourced from McCarthy (2019).

Now, there are a lot of factors at play here. And given the breadth of this study, making a blanket statement like "just work less and you'll make more money" is ignorant. But, at a minimum, this data tells us that being productive isn't all about jamming more hours into our workday, which is far too easy to do.

When we run into a problem, it's easy to throw more resources at it. Running behind for a meeting? Hit the gas and make up the lost time. Getting behind on a project? Hire someone else to pick up the slack. Push. Drive. Be aggressive. Sleep less. Work more. Never stop grinding. Never stop hustling. Never relent. It's a mindset all too pervasive in our country, especially in corporate America.

One winter, at a company retreat, our CEO gathered us to welcome an employee back from medical leave. Though this employee's condition was quite serious, she had returned to full health and full working capacity after a few weeks in the ER. We all clapped for her. We felt relieved for this person. We felt proud that the CEO took time to recognize her humanity. Had the CEO stopped there, I'd be singing his praises to this day. But the CEO (unfortunately) had more to say. He continued by stating how great it was that this employee, even in the midst of the worst medical emergency of her life, worked from her hospital bed. He praised her for keeping her laptop on hand and ready to respond to colleagues and customers at a moment's notice. The employee blushed with satisfaction, and everyone else took note; even if you're down and out, you sure as hell better keep working. At the very least, for praise and recognition. And at most, for job security or an overall sense of self-worth.

Stories like this are disappointing but all too common. Likely because we feel pressured to keep on working and hustling. And when we do, we're occasionally rewarded with praise, personal satisfaction, and accomplishment. So, like a pigeon that eventually finds a seed in a pile of pebbles, we keep pecking, searching for success, using the same strategy to solve the same problem, but mostly coming up with rocks in our mouth.

While it may seem counterintuitive, the data shows that creating more value doesn't mean working longer. Being productive isn't about grinding as much as possible. Success doesn't come from burning the candle at both ends, and well-being isn't associated with single-mindedly focusing on work. Even if it were, you can't be productive forever. Which leads us to Myth #2.

Myth #2 — You Can Stay Productive Forever, Just Like Those Instagram Stars

If you've spent even a minute on Instagram, you've seen a dozen influencers pushing the hustle and grind culture. They post selfies at the gym at 4 a.m. They share their 42-point morning routine complete with meditation and gratitude journaling. Then they celebrate their success, which came from working a 20-hour day before hitting the sack and doing it all again tomorrow. They glorify the push. They put "never stop" up on a pedestal. They market the idea that they're successful because they never quit and never give up. But they are lying by omission.

They omit the fact that, to wake up at 4 a.m. and exercise for two hours, they have to go to bed at 8 or 9 p.m. They skip sharing the days that don't go as planned. They auto-post pictures of success while stuck in traffic trying to get home to sick kids and unable to be productive in the least.

These influencers misinterpret the meaning of productivity. They don't share the truth that there's a balance between working hard, staying focused, and recovering. They're scared to admit that they can't always be productive; that they don't have the energy to work 24/7. Even if they did, they seem to ignore the science showing that our ability to perform at high levels requires us to change scenery from time to time.

> "In a society that judges self-worth on productivity, it's no wonder we fall prey to the misconception that the more we do, the more we're worth."
>
> — Ellen Sue Stern

According to the University of Illinois at Urbana-Champaign, our brain gets bored with unchanging circumstances, killing our productivity completely. Researchers showed that staring at the same document, driving down the same road, or focusing on the same project for too long hinders your ability to think creatively and get work done. In their words, "prolonged attention to a single task actually hinders performance," while "even brief diversions from a task can dramatically improve one's ability to focus on that task for prolonged periods" (Barlett, 2018).

So, just as we must make pit stops during a long car ride to eat, shake off the boredom, and stretch our legs, so too must we acknowledge that pushing 24/7 like the Instagram celebs pretend to do doesn't help, it hurts. After all, what's the use in constantly hustling if those extra work hours aren't helping you get more done?

Myth #3 — Do What the Billionaires Do and Success Will Follow

It's far too easy for any imbecile on the Internet to misrepresent their success. Take selfies on a beach, share pics of your dinner out, post big smiling photos of yourself at semi-exotic locations and you too can present the so-called perfect life to your followers. Anyone can talk the talk.

What about the *real* rich folk though? What about the people who have demonstrated massive financial success and truly have the means to live a posh life? Can we incorporate the tools and techniques they use to be productive and find our own success?

Years back, I got caught up following the advice of successful people on the Interwebs. I listened to their podcast interviews, read articles about their daily routines, and took notes on the way they lived. Before I knew it, I was waking up early, eating protein, drinking a tall glass of water, and taking a cold shower first thing in the morning. My thought was, if I followed the routines of these billionaires, financial windfall would be right around the corner. It wasn't.

My mistake was, as I detailed in Chapter One, following the tips and tricks of people who were *already* financially successful instead of the tips and tricks of someone who was *on their way* to be. What works for one won't work for the other. Case in point, many of the things I do today *aren't* the things that contributed to my success years ago. I exercise daily, eat a lot of protein, and journal. I'm also wealthier than I used to be. But those facts aren't correlated. In fact, I didn't exercise, track protein intake, or journal at all when I first started my career. Instead, I grew myself and my business with a plan; a process for getting things done, a method for achieving goals, and by working on things that mattered, all while maintaining my values so as not to unbalance my family and personal life.

Being a billionaire doesn't mean you are productive, and being productive won't make you a billionaire. Billionaires became billionaires because they had specific knowledge at a specific time in specific circumstances that led them down a specific path.

Your path is different. The mountains you wish to scale are different. Your circumstances and knowledge and challenges are all different. Which means *you* get to define what success means to you, and it doesn't have to be money.

Chapter Three

The Truths of Productivity

> "Should you find yourself in a chronically leaking boat, energy
> devoted to changing vessels is likely to be more productive than
> energy devoted to patching leaks."
>
> — Warren Buffett

Just Do It. I Will. Impossible is Nothing. These are the slogans of three trendy sports brands. They embody the idea of hard work, dedication, and an uncompromising attitude toward getting things done. This attitude bleeds beyond sports and into the business world. I know all too well.

Having worked in corporate America for nearly 20 years, an aggressive, can-do, never-take-no-for-an-answer attitude isn't just valued, it's expected. So when we don't finish everything we hope to, when we set goals and don't meet them, or when we have ambitions that aren't realized, we either get punished by our employers, punish ourselves with guilt, or both.

Science tells us that productivity is a complicated dance between the chemicals in your body giving you energy and the circumstances of your day that consume it. As such, using our willpower to be more productive is neither logical nor reasonable, which brings us to our first truth.

Truth #1 – Productivity is More Than Just Willpower

All humans naturally produce a motivation and happiness drug called dopamine, a feel-good chemical for your brain. Dopamine encourages you to take small risks and experience new things. Dopamine may have been the necessary neurotransmitter responsible for inspiring early humans to explore new places, even when the safety of their original habitation was more certain (Santos, 2018). In other words, without dopamine, it's possible that humanity would still be living in the rock huts we were first conceived.

Dopamine is incredibly influential to our productivity. If our dopamine levels are low, it's easier to procrastinate. We're less enthusiastic. We have more self-doubt. On the other hand, if our dopamine levels are high, we can increase our focus, attention, and concentration—all of which are critical factors for productivity. With high dopamine levels, we don't need the instant gratification that checking email or social media provides. We aren't as easily tempted by distraction, and we're willing to work a bit harder for bigger rewards.

According to Professor Wolfram Schultz who studies dopamine and the brain's reward centers at Cambridge University, the best way to release the most dopamine is with an unexpected reward. Conversely, the best way to withhold dopamine (which can frustrate and put you into a severe funk) is to set expectations that won't be met. Experientially, I know this to be true. My kids get wildly excited when we surprise them with a trip out for ice cream (unexpected reward = dopamine hit). But the times we've promised them ice cream and then change plans, all hell breaks loose (expected reward withdrawn = dopamine withheld).

But professor Schultz's studies go further by showing that our brains release dopamine not only when we get what we want, but just by wanting anything at all. The very act of desiring a treat, award, or goal creates the expectation of receiving or achieving that thing, which causes our brains to release dopamine, rewarding our good intentions.

Unfortunately, longer-term investments like exercise, reading self-help books, or finding a mentor won't do the trick. When your brain can't expect a reward somewhat immediately, it doesn't release dopamine. Worse, if you've forced yourself to get started but aren't seeing immediate results, your brain withholds dopamine because your high expectations weren't met, putting you into a funk that brings all further self-improvement to a halt. You won't feel good about what you're doing and will quickly fall back into old habits.

All of this is to say that productivity is more than just willpower. There are very real chemical and psychological factors at play. Simply "willing" ourselves to get shit done won't cut it. Yes, a certain amount of can-do attitude will benefit any venture. But as we've already seen, even the best can-do attitude only works for so long before it's time to take a break.

Many of the methods in this book aim to increase your dopamine and energy levels naturally, which in turn will increase your productivity. For example, you can positively affect your brain chemistry and productivity levels by merely jotting down an action item (releasing dopamine) and checking it off once finished (releasing more). As we'll see later, the mind, body, and spirit hacks in Part V will do the same. In fact, after you've built your system and begin using it, your energy tank will be consistently full. You'll be getting shit done and feeling good about it—before, during, and after—all without the enemy...

Truth #2 – Distraction is the Enemy

Baby sea turtles hatch by the hundreds, and usually at night. When they do, they have only one goal: get to the ocean as quickly as possible. This is complicated by the fact that baby turtles can barely see. They're forced to rely on big bright lights to guide their way. Moonlight reflecting off of the ocean works best. But when the moon isn't out and the beachfront is littered with houselights and flashlight-handling night walkers, mass confusion sets in.

My family and I witnessed this firsthand during one moonless night in Topsail, North Caroline. Hundreds of baby turtles hatched, waddled down the dune, and skittered all over the sand. They didn't know which way to go. Every house light was a distraction that would never lead them to their goal. Every flashlight put their very lives at risk.

It might seem dramatic to think that our own lives are at stake, but it's true. While we may not be in immediate danger of being eaten by a crab, getting lost in distraction is wasting away the only non-renewable resource we have—time. It's with this in mind that I can confidently drop our second productivity truth-bomb: distraction is the enemy.

Like a baby sea turtle following a house light on the beach, tasks that aren't aligned with our goals lead us nowhere. We waste precious time and energy pursuing "shiny objects" that hold the promise of a better life but will never move us closer to our goal nor will provide us with any level of personal or professional satisfaction. Distractions, though they appear to be real work, are devilishly disguised productivity killers. Above all else, we must stay focused on our main goals by freeing up time otherwise spent on distractions. And time is something we have more of than we think.

Truth #3 – You've Got More Time Than You Think

As is usually the case, the constant lure of people, devices, and events can keep us from working on what matters. This daily onslaught of activity can pull us in every direction, making it not only feel but actually *be* impossible to make progress toward our goals. We're often not aware of such distractions. Like a dog on a walk, we forget where we're going and what we're doing when a rabbit darts across our path. Each distraction pulls us ever so slightly in a different direction. Before we know it, 1,000 tasks have pulled us in 1,000 different directions, and every step we take is a step down the wrong path. This is best illustrated in "Essentialism" by Greg McKeown (2014):

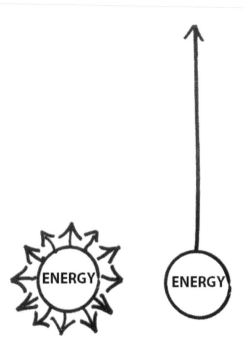

After sleep, exercise, eating, commuting, and meetings, any remaining time disappears in a fog. We neither know where it goes nor understand how to get it back.

Of course, this buffer time doesn't disappear. It's lost to distractions like news, social media, television, and other interruptions. Though small on their own, every article, email, and glance at your phone adds up. A survey conducted by the Global Web Index showed that, as of January 2019, Internet users are spending an average of two hours and 22 minutes per day on social media alone, up from one hour and 30 minutes in 2012 (Metev, 2019). At that rate, you're spending over 16 hours a week, 70 hours per month, and 863 hours per year. That's 8,630 hours over a decade—nearly an entire year doing nothing but scrolling through pictures of other people, liking their shit, and making witty comments to stroke your ego with likes from friends and family. This illustrates the importance of getting a handle on where our time is going, which is easily done using the following Time Pie exercise.

Below is a pie divided up into 24 slices. Each slice represents one hour of your day. On any given day, significant activities like the ones mentioned above—sleeping, exercising, eating, commuting, and meetings—will take up one or more slices of that pie. Go ahead and fill it out now. I have a point to make, and it won't make sense until you see how your time is divvied up. If you don't want to write in this book, download and print out the free Time Pie Worksheet at www.michaelmehlberg.com/homeearly.

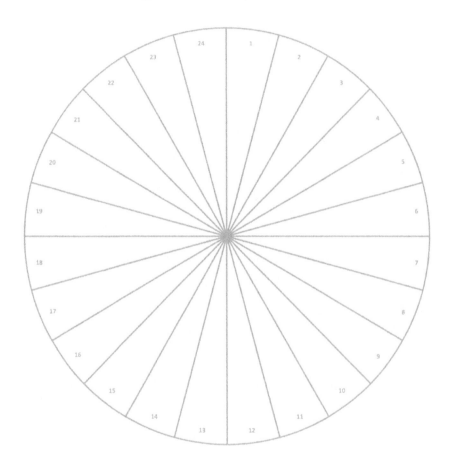

As you fill it out, consider every activity that takes up your time. Since sleep usually consumes the most, start there:

Sleep

Most Americans get between six and seven hours of sleep per night (Kennedy, 2015). Most people need between six and eight hours. How much do you currently average? Fill in the number of slices, labeling them "sleep" along the outer edge.

Commuting

The average American commutes 43.89 minutes (.73 hours) to and from work every day ("Become a Corporate Drone," n.d.). How about you? Fill in the number of slices and label them "commute" along the outer edge. Keep them adjacent to your sleep slices. When you've filled in every activity, you want one big block representing the remaining time available.

Eating

Most people spend 37 minutes per day traveling to get food, preparing to eat, and actually eating (Hamrick, 2016). Like you did for sleeping and commuting, fill your eating time in, labeling it "eating." If it takes 30 minutes to prepare and eat breakfast, another 30 for lunch, and an hour for dinner, that's two slices of your time pie. This may change from time to time, and that's okay. We just need the average for now.

Exercise

Most people spend 17 minutes exercising, on average (Romero, 2012). What about you? If you don't exercise, we'll discuss how important it is to your productivity in Chapter Seventeen. For now, fill in the number of slices representing how much you exercise on a given day. Be sure to factor in every aspect including getting dressed, driving to and from your gym, and any post-workout cleanup. For an activity like exercise where you might not do it every day, fill in the average number of hours you spend on days you do, and ignore the days you don't.

Work and Meetings

We're going to separate work from meetings because meetings are tricky. They can come and go depending on the day. To account for them, isolate the average number of meetings you have on a given day from the rest of your work time. For example, if you usually work an eight-hour day and have two hours of meetings, color two slices for meetings and six for work. Most people spend an hour per day in meetings and nearly an hour per day preparing for them (Mørch, 2017). If you have a more consistent nine to five job without much flex time, just fill in the total number of hours you typically work.

Other things to capture in your time pie include:

• Time taken getting dressed/ready for work

• Time shuttling kids around to school, practices, friends, etc.

• Time spent with your family

• Time spent on household activities

• Time spent on hobbies, leisure activities, or side-hustles

Here's what the average American's looks like:

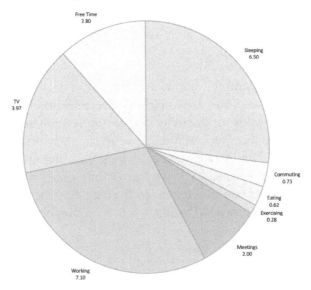

Like you, every person on this planet has the same 24 hours in their day. Their time pie will look different than yours. What do you notice about your time pie? What sticks out to you? Were the results what you expected? Does it appear you have extra time unaccounted for? If you're like many, you'll find blank slices of time. Maybe even four hours or more of extra time in your day.

When I first worked through this exercise myself, I was shocked to find almost four extra hours in my day. Had you asked me before the exercise, I would have told you that every moment of my day was packed, and I had no time for anything else. But my time pie told me that I was sitting around like a bump on a log. Of course, that wasn't true. Those extra hours represented the distractions in my life. Twenty minutes on Facebook, another twenty on Instagram, five on Twitter, and many untold hours of online shopping. It all added up. Once I visualized those hours, I knew I should apply them to more important activities.

Now, a few of us won't have extra time at the end of this exercise. If this is you, you need to build some buffer into your life. You're not going to masochistically pack your day with constant activity. You need to get clarity on what's most important and reallocate the time necessary to make progress toward it. That means killing or reducing some of the activities in your Time Pie. We'll do exactly this in Part IV.

Finally, regardless of whether you have extra time or are scheduled to the max, you need to balance your day. This means applying the appropriate amount of time to each area in your life based on your priorities and values. For example, if your family is priority number one but you spend only fifteen minutes with them before bed, you may be out of balance. Or, if you prioritize your health and fitness but never take time to exercise, the scales are tipped too far in the wrong direction. In life, some activities (work, for example) get out of whack and take the focus away from other important areas of your life. Spend too long in this unbalanced state and you'll begin to resent the activities that steal time away from what you value most.

"The proper function of man is to live, not to exist. I shall not waste my days in trying to prolong them. I shall use my time."

— Jack London

We'll work toward balancing your portfolio of activities in Chapter Twenty-One. For now, I simply want this Time Pie exercise to show you that, though you may *feel* slammed to the max, you've got more time than you think. Of course, what you do with that time is the ultimate exercise. We all have 24 hours in a day. It's how we choose to use it that distinguishes one person from the next. Rest assured; Warren Buffet isn't blowing two hours scrolling through his Instagram feed every day. He's focused on what matters to him. Which brings us to our final truth.

Truth #4 – Your Why Matters

Simon Sinek popularized the idea of a Golden Circle with his viral Ted Talk, *How Great Leaders Inspire Action* (Sinek, 2010). The Golden Circle is a framework has been used by some of the most successful companies, including Apple, Inc. to build inspiring, winning, and lasting organizations.

The Golden Circle is a three-ring target. The outer ring is your company's *what*, explaining what products you sell, what services you provide, and what help you offer. The middle ring is your company's *how*, describing how you do what you do and how your organization is different from the competition. The center of the Golden Circle is your company's *why*. It's your company's purpose, its belief, its cause, its reason for being.

Every company understands *what* they do. A few know *how* they are different. But, only a minuscule number of companies understand *why* they do what they do and believe what they believe. Those companies are the unicorns—few and far between, but wildly beautiful and successful.

This Golden Circle applies to productivity also. Most of us know *what* we're doing. Many of us even know *how* we'll do it. But the few of us who know *why* we do what we do will rarely be lost to distraction. This *why* is our purpose. And, purpose gives us clarity, drive, and personal fulfillment. It makes us grateful and allows us to redefine success on our terms.

To be clear, goals and purpose are not the same. Many of us have goals, and those goals are important. But they're not enough. Goals set you on a path that will one day end. If your goal succeeds, your purpose will help you set bigger goals and keep your momentum. If your goal fails, your purpose will help you recover from it.

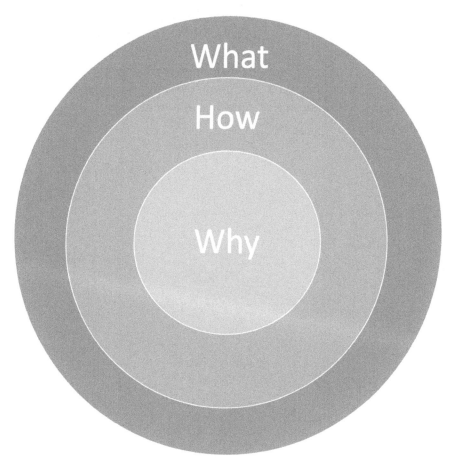

Figure: *Simon Sinek's Golden Circle*

Like anyone, my past is riddled with both successes and failures. The failures used to stall me completely. Like the time I tried to learn piano only to realize it would take far longer than a month to sound like George Winston playing the Charlie Brown theme song. But successes used to stall me too. Like the time I developed and published a successful iPhone app only to quickly lose interest in building what was sure to be a thriving business around it. Or the time I passed a three-day training course and studied 1,600 pages of material on computer security only to skip taking the certification test.

My goals were clear, so I knew whether I had succeeded or failed. But once that success or failure hit, there was nothing left for me to do. Without a clear purpose, there was nowhere left for me to go.

Your why matters. Goals that aren't aligned with your purpose only have you working hard on tasks that ultimately don't matter. As such, starting with your purpose is paramount to being your most productive self. It's also the beginning of our journey herein.

Chapter Four

Beginning the Journey

"You see, in life, lots of people know what to do, but few people actually do what they know. Knowing is not enough! You must take action."

— Tony Robbins

We've now defined a few questions to answer over the course of this book: What is meaningful to us? How can we make time for it? And once we get started, how can we prevent distractions and urgent matters from compromising our most important work? The answer to all three questions is building a system based on the science of productivity and the evidence for how *you* perform. We'll start with *your* purpose, *your* why, and what matters to *you*.

Once you uncover your driving principles, we will work to define a vision for your life, set goals to realize that vision, and create a habit management system for continually accelerating your progress and success. Finally, we'll look at scientifically proven ways to use sleep, exercise, nutrition, music, and even plants to avoid distractions and optimize your day so that you can get home early.

And getting home early is the goal here. That's why you picked up this book. It's not that you want to be lazy, avoid responsibility, or earn a paycheck for doing nothing. Sure, we all joke about such things, but that wouldn't match your integrity or work ethic. No, the reason for getting home early is precisely because you *do* want to work hard. You *want* to give it your all, make a difference, and get shit done. But you also want to live a balanced life. You want to spend time with your spouse, play with your children, travel, and have time for a hobby or two on the side. Hell, you may even have ambitions of starting a business, writing a book, coaching your kids' baseball team, or helping others through volunteering. You can't do any of that if you're stuck in an office late at night, working on "just one more task" before heading home. Nor can you do that if you finish your workday cranky and devoid of energy and motivation.

#

Make no mistake, when you're done reading this book, your life won't look appreciably different. That's right; this book isn't going to change your life on its own. You'll just know more. But, as G.I. Joe used to say, "knowing is half the battle." And once you know, *you* need to charge into the other half of the battle. *You* will need to implement the knowledge you've gained and the system you've created here. Then *you* will need to follow it.

If you implement the system in this book, you'll become a different person. You'll be that someone who has their life in order. You'll know exactly what goals you're trying to hit and how you'll get there. You'll have a plan for how you'll start, what you'll work on during, and how you'll finish each and every day.

Those may sound like high expectations for a book. But you should have high expectations for this book because you should have high expectations for yourself. By the time you reach the end, you'll have built a system to use every year, every month, every week, and every day to get the most out of your time. You'll find yourself working on what matters. You'll rise with fire, knowing that between breakfast and dinner, you'll be able to work toward your purpose. After a year, I hope you will look back in amazement at what you've accomplished, and look forward to an even better, more organized, more productive year to come.

How to Read This Book

This book is not a collection of random life-hacks. Sure, if you want to know how caffeine affects productivity, you can jump right to that section and read it. But be warned, any tools, tips, and tricks you find herein are the equivalent of reading random productivity articles on the web; though the advice may work for some people, it will likely not work for you in a vacuum. However, if you come across a productivity tip and you understand how to apply it to the system we'll build together, you will begin to see real benefits and results.

And when I say, "build a system," I mean it. You're gonna have to do the work. Armed with only the knowledge you obtain from reading this book, you might end up a halfway decent productivity coach. But if you actually do the work, build the system, and apply these lessons to your life, you'll realize the benefits that brought you here in the first place: destroying distraction, focusing on what matters, achieving your goals, realizing your vision, and living your purpose.

I see this book as a reference for important milestones in your life. It's a book you can use time and again to refine your vision, achieve your goals, and continually make progress to what's important. So, while I recommend you read this through from cover to cover the first time, I also recommend you refer to individual sections in the future. It will come in useful when you accomplish your goals and need to set new ones, or when you find that what's important to you has changed and you need another round of purpose and vision discovery.

And don't be surprised if that happens. It will, likely more than once in your life. Right now, for example, finishing and publishing this very book matters most to me. Of course, if you're reading it, my big goal has been fulfilled. Does that mean I sit on the couch and eat peanut M&M's all day, turning into a useless slob? No, and when you've achieved your goals, neither should you.

Rather, once you've achieved your goals, come back to this book and use its principles to refine your purpose and vision, set new goals, and create a plan for your future, just like you'll do now.

PART II

Looking Back from the Future

From disorganized overwhelm to purposefully productive

"Life is long enough, and a sufficiently generous amount has been given to us for the highest achievements if it were all well invested."
— Seneca

^ Translation: You've got plenty of time to achieve anything, if you focus.

Chapter Five

Purpose Driven Productivity

> "It is not enough to be busy...the question is: what are we busy about?"
>
> — Henry David Thoreau

My first computer was made by Zenith, a company that went under decades ago. I'm not sure why our family bought one. Back in the '90s, computers were both ridiculously expensive and equally useless. Regardless, we cleared our finest desk and displayed it prominently in our family room where I got to work falling in love with it. Not just for games like Reader Rabbit, Math Blaster, and Carmen San Diego, but for its ability to be programmed.

I would sit for hours, creating useless programs to exercise control over the machine. Around 1992 we received a Prodigy Online CD in the mail. Remember American Online? Prodigy was a precursor to AOL, the eventual king of online services. Though the Internet, at that time, consisted of a few underwhelming bulletin boards run out of people's garages, I was hooked. Having learned how to program some basic applications, I was both confounded and thrilled by the complexity of connecting my Zenith via telephone to computers hundreds of miles away.

My fascination with computers grew to become the driving force behind my every thought. I made friends who understood computers. I sought out jobs that revolved around computers. Eventually, I built an entire career on them. For two decades, computers would be my guiding light. A north star of sorts.

zenith [**zee**-nith *or, esp. British*, **zen**-ith] SHOW IPA 🔊

SEE SYNONYMS FOR *zenith* ON THESAURUS.COM

noun

1   the point on the celestial sphere vertically above a given position or observer.: Compare nadir.

2   a highest point or state; culmination.

Figure: *Definition of Zenith from* www.dictionary.com.

Fittingly, the word Zenith was more than a cool computer name. I learned in a college Astronomy course years later that a zenith was the point directly above the north pole. The word itself means the highest point, the top, the pinnacle. There was no doubt that computers had become my zenith. And that made personal growth and productivity extremely simple. I never wondered what to read or do. Every decision I made revolved around whether it would help me learn more about computers or not. In short, it made being productive a breeze.

#

As I'd come to realize, being truly productive in any endeavor requires this type of overarching direction in our lives. Without a guiding light, we will simply drift from one task to the next, unsure of where we're going or what we're doing. We'll work hard, hustle, and get shit done. But that shit won't help move us toward our goals. Our effort will be directionless, making it difficult to focus and grow. A guiding light helps us understand what matters. And when you realize what matters, you know exactly what to do (and what not to).

If you don't know what matters, you can work on anything—emails, text messages, or video games—and feel productive. But if none of these things matter, you're not growing. You're just wasting your only non-renewable resource: time.

"When a man lacks guiding principles, his attention mindlessly pivots to whatever the world tells him is important, and typically what the world tells him is important is corrosive to a truly flourishing life."

— Brett MacKay, Art of Manliness

Of course, the ultimate guiding light is your life's purpose, which is not something all of us have found. While we may have strong interests, as I did with computers, an absolute reason for being is harder to nail down. If you can find it, that guiding light will help you be purposefully productive for the rest of your life. But even if you can't, having purpose in the seven major areas in your life is incredibly powerful, and easy to define (more on this in a bit).

I'll admit finding your purpose sounds a little woo-woo, a little new age. But there's a reason it's so powerful: when driven by purpose, you experience dozens of immediate, practical, life-changing benefits. In a National Institute of Health study performed in 1998, researchers found that people with purpose lived up to seven years longer than people without ("The Right Outlook," n.d.). In a 2013 Gallup/Healthways study, having a purpose has been shown to double the likelihood that you'll learn something new every day. This same study concluded that you'll increase your likelihood of being engaged at work by 400%. Multiple Neilson studies have shown that customers will pay more for a product with a purpose and are more likely to select a product with a purpose over one without ("What Scientific Studies Show," n.d.). Not to mention, 7 out of 10 millennials want to work for a company with a purpose (Craig & Snook, 2014).

Imagine what you could do with seven extra years. Imagine how much faster you could accelerate your career if you were more engaged than your peers at work. Imagine running a company that makes more money and has a better talent pool to hire from than your competition.

It would be wildly rewarding. Which just goes to show how much we all crave purpose, either for ourselves or others. And, like a business that makes more money or hires better employees, if we are clear enough on our purpose, we'll receive more of what we want and surround ourselves with more people who will help us become a better version of ourselves.

Longer life, faster learning, better engagement, and more money. Sounds too good to be true. But the benefits don't end there. Beyond these studies, I've found that purpose gives you both tangible and intangible tools to find balance and fulfillment:

Purpose Gives You Clarity

With one fundamental driving force behind your actions, there's no question whether the task you're working on will help or hurt. Everything you do will clearly support your purpose, or not. Before getting started on any task or project, you'll know whether you'll be wasting your time or using it wisely.

Purpose Gives You Focus

With a guiding light to follow, it's easy to eliminate distractions and remain single-mindedly focused on that which matters. You'll immediately recognize a distraction for what it is, something that takes you away from working toward your purpose.

Purpose Gives Your Life Meaning

When you know your destination, anything you do that helps you get there is fulfilling. The progress you make, no matter how small, will mean something. It will be worth celebrating because you will know exactly what you're working for.

Purpose Fills and Fulfills You

Loading your day with meaningful, purpose-driven activities fills you up with energy, happiness, and satisfaction. You'll be excited to get to work and, once your work is done, you'll be energized by what you've accomplished.

Purpose Gives You Drive

When you have somewhere to go and something to do, there's no use sitting around. Your purpose will sit at the forefront of every activity (or non-activity), beckoning you to take action, inspiring you to grow.

Purpose Redefines Success on Your Terms

Your purpose will be unique to you, and no one else. Since your ultimate objective is something only you can do, the limitations and expectations of others don't matter. *You* get to define how you achieve success. *You* get to choose how you succeed.

Finally, Purpose Makes You Grateful

When you live up to and for your purpose, there are no regrets, no second guesses. Only clear, focused, meaningful, and fulfilling action driving you to success on your terms. If you didn't have anything for which to be grateful before, with purpose, you will.

#

You might be thinking, "this purpose thing sounds nice but isn't for me. I have goals. I have drive. And, I have to pay the bills." But remember, we're not talking about your life's purpose here. We're talking about having a purpose to drive each *area* of your life. Purpose, even for your nine to five job, has massive benefits. And goals simply aren't enough.

As we saw in the last chapter, The Truth of Productivity, goals are helpful, practical, and useful. People who set goals (and write them down) have been shown in study after study to be more likely to achieve them (Economy, 2018). In fact, this book has two whole chapters dedicated to proper goal setting, tracking, and executing. But if you don't set the right goal, you'll simply waste your time and sap yourself of energy. That's where purpose comes in.

For example, if you've set a goal to become a pilot in your off time but your purpose is to inspire others to live a healthy life by running marathons, you'll fly to victory but die on the road. If your purpose is to teach others through writing but you set a goal of selling $1 million for your business, you may succeed in selling but never write a book that will change people's lives. Goals, when not aligned with your purpose, will distract you from doing what's necessary to live a life of meaning. It's the very reason so many who find financial success aren't happy. They're winning at making money but failing at life.

Furthermore, a goal sets you on a path that will one day end either in failure or success. If your goal ends in failure, you'll be left wondering how to recover. If it ends in success, you'll be left wondering what to do next. Purpose is the one thing that will guide you through failure, help you recover from it, and help you set new goals to move on. Purpose is the one thing that will keep you moving and growing long after you succeed.

#

As I said before, if you don't know your *life's* purpose, that's okay. Few people do, or ever will. Luckily, you don't need one to build a productivity system that gets you home early. Instead of finding your *life's* purpose, we can focus on finding purpose in seven fundamental aspects of life—your friends and family, your wealth and finances, your spiritual and self, your hobbies and side-hustles, your attitude and character, your career and business, and your health and fitness. And while this means you'll need to craft more than one purpose statement, each one will be smaller, more focused, and far easier to define.

Health and Fitness

What does healthy mean to you? How fit do you want to be? Do you want a sculpted body or to be strong as an ox? Do you want a low resting heart rate? Whatever the answer, ask yourself, why?

I want to be extremely strong and sculpted. Not because I'm a dude. Because I'm tall and skinny, I have always struggled to build muscle, and I know that doing so will require me to push myself, push my boundaries, and expect more out of myself than I ever have in the past. So, I set out on a challenging lifting routine that would push those boundaries. I knew that, gaining muscle while keeping trim would require both physical and mental strength. Every day I moved closer to that goal would build the mindset and fortitude to accomplish more in every other aspect of my life.

What's your why for health and fitness? Why do you want the health and fitness goals you've set for yourself? Write that down and make it your Health and Fitness Purpose.

_____

_____

_____

_____

_____

If you'd rather not write in this book, are back to perform this exercise again, or want to share this with friends and family, download my Purpose Worksheet at www.michaelmehlberg.com/homeearly.

Friends and Family

What do you want for your friends and family? How do you want to interact with them? How do you want to treat them? How do you want them to treat you? Now, with all that in mind, ask yourself, why?

I want my wife to love me, see me, respect me. I want my kids to listen to me, love me, respect me. I want to teach my children how I see the world while encouraging them to develop their own thoughts and views. I want my children to be knowledgeable, have uncompromising morals and values, and find their purpose in life. Why? Because I love to teach others. I love to be seen and heard. Because deep down, I want my children to grow up and see the world as an amazing place, in a fantastic time, worthy of their attention and ready for their ideas and leadership.

What's your *why* for your friends and family? Write it down. That will be your Friends and Family Purpose.

_____

_____

_____

_____

_____

Wealth and Finances

It sounds nice to have a private yacht, a helicopter, a garage full of Lamborghini's, and a 50,000 square foot mansion on an island in the pacific. But we don't often strive to get those things. Not only because we don't need them, but because when we ask ourselves why, the answer isn't powerful enough to justify the work required to earn them.

What lifestyle do you want to live? How much money do you need to live that lifestyle? How much do you want to have saved for your retirement, for a rainy day, for your kids' college funds? Then, ask yourself why?

For me, I'd like to live an upper-middle-class lifestyle where we don't have to think about money when we do normal activities. If we made millions of dollars per year, that would be great, but we wouldn't change the way we live. Why? Because we know what we like and how we want to live. We don't want to be among the wealthy and famous.

We want to keep our midwestern values and friends while not wanting for cash. We want our kids to have college available to them if that's what they want for their future. We want to have at least six months of salary in the bank for a rainy day. And, we want to have the option to retire at 60 years old and live the rest of our lives with the same lifestyle as we enjoy today.

What's the lifestyle you want to achieve? How much do you want saved for financial expenses in the future? Then, ask yourself why? Write it down and make that your Wealth and Finances Purpose.

_____

_____

_____

_____

_____

Spiritual and Self

How do you want to exercise your deeper, inner, perhaps spiritual or religious side? What do you want to learn? How do you want to grow? Why?

I want to participate in church weekly, listening to its message for clarity and meaning. I want to hear their perspective on life and the world. I wish to inform my philosophical side with thoughtful books and self-improvement advice. Why? Because my religion has thought deeply about a side of life that I cannot see or hear or feel or touch, and many of the values they teach are values I'd love to instill in my children.

How does your spiritual or self-growth matter to you, and why? Write it down and let that be your Spiritual and Self Purpose.

_____

_____

_____

_____

_____

Career and Business

You have career goals. Maybe it's to work at another company. Perhaps it's to get a promotion, be recognized by your peers, or manage people. What are those goals? Keeping them in mind, ask yourself why?

My career goals include leading a marketing and sales department, growing our companies' business, being recognized as an instrumental asset to the company by my peers and boss. Why? Because I love finding the truth in technology products and helping people understand that truth in creative ways that help them solve their problems. Also, because I'm patriotic, and I love the feeling of helping our men and women in uniform with my technology skills.

Are you in the right career? If so, where do you want to take it? If not, what is your ideal career and why? Write down why, making that your Career and Business Purpose.

_____

_____

_____

_____

_____

Hobbies and Side-Hustles

Most people work for money. That work isn't always their passion or purpose. I'm a corporate weenie doing business development, marketing, and sales with a passion for writing (hence this book). I know another corporate employee who is a graphic designer, a grocery store clerk who is a fitness trainer, and a professor running a winery on the side. In this day in age, hobbies and side-hustles abound. What's your side-hustle, and why? Why do you want to consume valuable time working more after working a full day? For me, I write to learn about new subjects and get clear on my thoughts while teaching others and, hopefully, make a bit of scratch along the way.

What is your hobby or side-hustle? Ask yourself, why is it important to you? Why do you do it? Write that down as your Hobbies and Side-Hustles Purpose.

_____

_____

_____

_____

_____

Attitude and Character

In grade school, our counselors spent a lot of time helping us figure out *what* we would do once we entered the "real world." But nobody ever asked us *who* we wanted to be, which, in retrospect, seems like a more important question to ask. Case in point, we've all heard of (and may even know some) highly paid professionals who lack integrity, have a terrible attitude, and generally dislike people. On the other hand, there are underpaid teachers who light up the world. They each chose their profession, but the teacher decided *who* to be and lives accordingly. Who do you want to be, and why?

I want to stand up for what's right. I want to be grounded, strong, and live with integrity. I want to be helpful without being a pushover. I want to say what I mean and mean what I say. I want to be well-spoken, have deep and logical thoughts about relevant domestic and foreign issues. I want to bring an empathetic attitude the world, one that imagines creative, smart, logical, and meaningful solutions to complicated problems. Why? Because these are the characteristics I value in others and want for myself. Living this way is deeply satisfying and, if I embody these characteristics, I know I'll reach the end of my life with no regrets.

What's the attitude and character you want to bring out into the world? Then, ask yourself, why? Write that down as your Attitude and Character Purpose.

_____

_____

_____

_____

_____

These are not easy questions to answer. But they are necessary. Living a productive life means focusing your effort on what matters. Since each of these seven areas of your life matter, defining a purpose for them will bring clarity to your every move. It will also lay the groundwork for defining your vision, which we'll do in the next chapter.

But not before we take a quick stab at finding an overarching purpose for your life; one that covers all seven life areas. This can be challenging, and you may not find answers right away, but it's an exercise you can come back to later while you carry on with building your productivity system throughout the rest of this book.

Life's Purpose Exercises

Over the years, I've read multiple books and articles on purpose. I've spent months agonizing over why computers weren't my guiding light anymore. I've wondered what my new guiding light should be and how it related to a deeper, more fundamental life-purpose that would inspire, guide, and drive me until the day I die. Along the way, I've used dozens of exercises to discover my purpose so I could get back to being productive. Some of those exercises were a waste of time, but others helped me get closer to the answer. What follows are the good ones. No single one worked, but, assuming you take the time to think deeply about each one, a combination of the following questions will help get you closer.

Purpose Question #1 — What if I died today?

If you were to die today, would you feel good about your life? If yes, ask yourself why. If no, ask yourself what would have been missing.

This question may seem a bit morbid, but we only get one chance here. By propelling ourselves to the moment our chance is over, we can sometimes realize the one thing we were put on the earth to do.

We don't always get the opportunity to do that one thing. We don't always get to move on without regrets. When the bills pile up, we can't start working on a passion project if it's not bringing home the bacon. We have to get back to our day job, and that's okay. But the question still applies. By putting our inevitable death within arm's reach, it can give us perspective on what is purposeful today.

Purpose Question #2 — How can I help others?

What do others want that you can help them get? What skills or expertise or resources can you bring to help solve someone else's problem(s)?

For me, it's the application of technology, science, and processes to living a productive and meaningful life. I love technology, am good at using it, and get asked to help others often. I also love listening to the problems people have and will go out of my way to offer advice for how they can deal with those problems using tools, technologies, or techniques I know.

In an age where we can have food delivered directly to our refrigerator from the comfort of our couch, it's easy to live like a hermit crab. But this life won't carry much meaning if it's not spent, at least in part, helping others. We can't be good at everything. And that's a good thing. If we were, we wouldn't be able to focus on the one thing we're put on this earth to do — your purpose.

Purpose Question #3 — What is my superpower?

Superman was put on this planet to be a beacon of hope in a world full of evil. We identify with him because he's vulnerable, but we looked up to him because he has powers we can only dream of.

You have powers too. Powers that others see as superpowers. What are they? What can you do that nobody else can? How do you currently use these powers to help others? How could you use your powers to help others more?

Purpose Question #4 — Who will I be in 20 years?

When you're first born, you have no idea what the first 20 years of your life will be like. It's too far out of your control. There are too many relationship and environmental variables that can change the entire course of your life against your will. But now, older, and sporting your own free will, you can ask yourself, what do you want to say you've accomplished 20 years from now?

Twenty years is a long time, but that's exactly the point. In 20 years, you could accomplish so much. You could make huge changes to your life and the lives of those around you. Thinking 20 years ahead takes your mind out of the day-to-day firefighting and places it far in the future with enough time to do or become almost anything. What accomplishments come to mind? What changes would you seek to make?

Purpose Question #5 — What if money were no issue?

Most of the time, we're consumed with making money. If we're not paying the bills, we're saving for retirement, college, or the next sexy Apple gadget. So we work. And we save. And we spend. And then we work some more.

That work pays but isn't always aligned with our purpose. But, ask yourself, if money were no issue, what would you do while you weren't concerned with making it?

If you inherited an absurd amount of money tomorrow, enough to buy an airplane and fly to an island on which you've built your perfect home and filled it with a staff of full-time housekeepers, chefs, and the like, what would you do with your time? If you had absolutely everything you'd ever need to live a rich and safe life, what would you build? Who would you spend time with?

Taking money out of the equation gives us the freedom to think about more than the next house payment. It lets us think about how we'd spend our time. If money were no issue, what would you do?

#

When you find your purpose, you'll know it. What you write down will feel natural, and the very sight of it will be energizing. You'll notice a pattern of activities and achievements in your past that apply to what you've captured on paper. You'll also come to find that you no longer need anyone's approval, anyone's encouragement, or anyone's inputs to live that purpose. You will feel compelled to do it on your own accord, with or without receiving payment.

If you don't feel good about what you've written, or if you want to ask yourself a few other questions to be certain you've found your purpose before moving on to other parts of this book, grab my full set of purpose worksheets at www.michaelmehlberg.com/homeearly. These have a bundle of questions you can ask yourself to further explore your reason for being. While you find it, you can move on with this book to define a detailed vision for your life and set goals to get there.

If your vision and goals need to change as you discover true north, no problem. You shouldn't think of this as a one-time exercise. My purpose has changed. Yours likely will too. Big life events like getting married, having kids, and switching jobs will undoubtedly have an effect. My purpose in school was programming computers. I spent every waking minute reading, learning, and practicing that art.

And, while that purpose guided me through college and a bit beyond, I'm no longer driven by it. I've found a different why—thinking, learning, and teaching through my writing—which I now focus my energy on with the same rigor and enthusiasm as my former self did on software engineering.

So, use these exercises now, and come back to them if you feel lost. Use them when your productivity wanes and you feel disconnected from your work. They will help you identify your zenith, that guiding light that you will always be able to see, always be able to keep in mind, and always be able to head toward. They will also lead you to step two, which is using your purpose to define a vision for your life.

Chapter Six

Looking Back from the Future

"The most pathetic person in the world is someone who has sight but no vision."

— Helen Keller

If your purpose is a star overhead illuminating your life's direction, your vision is the way you want to live as you sail toward it. If your purpose is *why* you get up in the morning, your vision is *how* you go about your day. Thinking back to Simon Sinek's three ring target, purpose/why is at the center, and vision/how is the next ring around it. Your vision is how you'd like to work toward that purpose.

My purpose is to write. My big goal in support of that purpose is to write this book. Having gone through the exercises outlined in the previous chapter, I know that if I were to die tomorrow without publishing these pages, my casket would be filled with regret. But neither regret, goals, nor purpose is enough to guide me. If it were, then writing a book from a jail cell while eating oatmeal steeped in toilet water would be fine. My meals would be taken care of, and I'd have relative solidarity to focus and concentrate on the task at hand. I'd get my book written, fulfill my purpose of writing, and be one happy inmate.

Of course, this is not the vision I have for my life. While writing a book is a huge driver for me, the life I envision isn't one behind bars. I'd like to wake up and plan my day (in cursive, on nice paper, with a fountain pen, over a cup of coffee). I'd like to clean up emails, check social media, browse the news, then shower and get ready. After that, I'd write my book. Not in a jail cell, but in my office over a second cup of coffee while listening to a good vinyl by candlelight. When I tire of that, I'd exercise, get cleaned up, then go back to writing until dinner. I'd occasionally procrastinate with some online shopping. At night I'd play games or watch movies with my family. I'd practice playing guitar or learning chess and end the day with a good fiction novel before seven and a half hours of sleep.

That's a vision. It integrates your purpose with how you want to live your day, your month, and your year. It defines how you'd like your life to look while striving to achieve what matters. While purpose is what makes a life worth living, your vision is how you actually want to live.

#

Like defining your purpose, defining your vision sounds like a wishy-washy, head-in-the-clouds, pie-in-the-sky activity. But after purpose, it's the most important thing you can do.

Without a vision, you may wake up to pursue your why, but dread the day to come. You may sacrifice important aspects of your life—family time, hobbies, etc.—in pursuit of your guiding light.

People without a vision are passing time in an ad-hoc manner. They're living, but not necessarily their own life. They may be distracted and misdirected by other people's wishes and desires. They're moved by the changing currents of society. The goals they set, if any, aren't aligned with how they want their life to turn out. They set goals for setting goals sake. They make money for making moneys sake. And when they achieve their goals and make their money, they don't feel as fulfilled or accomplished as they'd hoped.

People who have a vision are inspired by their work, their family, and their life because it's what they designed. Even if they're not living the way they want at the moment, they know where they want to go and so can create a path to get there.

So, let's craft a vision that you can live by. One that leaves you feeling both fulfilled and accomplished. We'll envision your perfect future; one in which every important aspect of your life is going exactly the way you want. To do that, let's run through a simple exercise of looking back from one year in the future.

Imagine Your Perfect Year

"You've got to give yourself the freedom to dream — to use your imagination to see and feel what does not yet exist. A vision is not the same as goals or objectives; those come from the head. A vision comes from the heart."

— John Graham

It's time to imagine your perfect year. A year in which everything went right, and you've charted a course to living your dreams. Write down what an amazing year would look like. What did you accomplish? How did you feel at the end of the year? How did other people feel about you? Why?

_____

_____

_____

_____

_____

_____

Be specific. And I mean really, very, extremely specific. Your vision can't be blurry. It can't be faded. It has to be crystal clear so you understand exactly where you want to go. That means ensuring your vision has clarity around those seven important aspects of your life. Aspects you'll envision now:

Health and Fitness

Remember, you're writing this from your own perspective: super successful, one year in the future. How did you feel about yourself throughout the year? Strong? Confident? Sexy? How often did you workout? How hard? What did you eat? What did you most enjoy about your health and fitness journey? How did others to perceive you? How have you changed from one year ago?

_____

_____

_____

_____

_____

Friends and Family

Who do you hang out with, and how often? How do you feel after spending time with these loved ones? How do they feel about you? How much time did you dedicate to those closest to you every day? How many vacations did you take with them? Where did you go? What did you do? What meaningful things did you do for each other?

_____

_____

_____

_____

_____

Wealth and Finances

How much money are you making? What are your sources of income? How much do you have invested? How much do you have saved? How do you feel about the money you have saved? Is it close to meeting your retirement goals? On track? How much money did you donate, and to what causes? Where do you spend most of your money? Where did you feel good about saving a buck? Where did you feel good about spending it?

_____

_____

_____

_____

_____

Spiritual and Self

Is this church for you? Or is it introspection and reflection? Or is it both? How often did you focus on this aspect of your life? How often did you pray? How often did you meditate? What things do you do, and what time or money do you give to nurture your inner self? What books did you read? Who did you learn from? What did your self-improvement journey look like throughout the year?

_____

_____

_____

_____

_____

Hobbies and Side-Hustles

Do you moonlight? What is your side-hustle, and how much time did you spend on it? How much money did you make, if any? What did you accomplish? How do you feel about what you've done and where your business is heading? What have you lined up to make next year even easier, even more productive?

_____

_____

_____

_____

Attitude and Character

How did you act? How do you feel? Confident? Strong? Loving? Did you stand up for something you believe in? How did you grow as a person? What did you learn? What do you know or believe now that you didn't believe a year ago? How do others perceive you differently in this new year?

_____

_____

_____

_____

_____

Career and Business

What did you accomplish? How much time did you spend? What did you learn and who did you learn from? How will those learnings inform you and help you achieve even more success in the coming year? Did you get a raise? A promotion? Good favor with a boss or an important colleague? Where can you get to now that you couldn't get to before?

_____

_____

_____

_____

This may seem like a lot, but don't let it overwhelm you. Just focus on crafting a picture of your ideal self: this person in the future that is working to fulfill his or her purpose. Imagine what every component of your life will look like along the way. It doesn't have to be right, and it doesn't have to be long. When I create mine at the end of every year, it ends up being around 300 words (just a few paragraphs). Here's mine from 2018, looking forward to 2019:

1-Year Vision

I wrote and published a book. It's selling great with rave reviews and driving people to my business Where I write every day and sell to my email list. I find it on bookshelves in bookstores and convenience stores which is fucking awesome.

I'm making $20-50k per month on affiliate links and book sales and speaking engagements and coaching. I've even got a second book in the works which will be ready to publish in 2020.

Twice a month, we go to church. Four times a year, we go on week-long vacations. Many Fridays, I take off or take off when the kids are out of school to go skiing or visit New York or some other fun.

I have great starts to every morning, journaling, sometimes meditating, eating and thinking and planning and getting ready for my day via candlelight, alone. I work out when I want, listen to audiobooks while exercising, and read real books over lunch.

At the end of the year, I'm feeling accomplished because I have focused on a simple, clear, working strategy to get subscribers, of which I now have 10k and which is growing rapidly. My business works, and I know how to work it, and I know how to make money and sustain.

I've invested over $X in stocks, have over $Y in cash assets, have $Z total being managed by my financial advisor.

Other people wonder what I do. The people who know what I do are always asking what I'm going to write next. They are intrigued. They want to know more. They want to read what I write.

I spent the year confident, standing up for what's right, making an impact on those around me. I'm listened to, respected, and inspiring. I'm full of life and energy.

5-Year Vision

Three books published. $3M in net worth. $50k monthly income. Self-employed. Healthy and respectful family. Strong as an ox, full of life, wise, and a trained leader.

I review this vision monthly (as part of the Monthly Retrospective we'll discuss in Chapter Twenty), sometimes modifying it to reflect what I've learned and how I've grown.

A Vision for Your Day

You can't live a perfect year if you don't have a vision for how you'd like every day in that year to go. If the majority of those 365 days are miserable, it's going to be a long slog. So, defining a vision for your days is just as important as defining what you want your life to look like one year out.

Defining your perfect day starts the night before with your bedtime routine. As we'll see in Chapter Sixteen, getting enough sleep is critical to staying clear and focused on what matters. As such, a vision for how much sleep you would like to get is step one. Notice I said how much you'd *like* to get; not how much you think you can afford. Remember, we're crafting our perfect day here, not rehashing an already exhausting day that starts with too little rest.

From there, ask yourself what your perfect morning looks like. What's the first thing you want to do when you wake up? What's the first thing that gives you energy and momentum for the long day ahead? Throughout this perfect day, what would you eat and drink? Who would you talk to, if anybody? Would you journal, meditate, or exercise first thing? Once your day is started, when would you start work? How long would you work? When would you break for lunch, and what would eat when you do? Think about when your workday would end and your ideal commute home. When would you arrive home? What kind of mood would you be in as you walked through the door? Would you eat dinner right away, hang with your family, visit friends, study, or play video games?

Just like with your one-year vision, define your perfect day in as great of detail as you can. The clearer you make your vision, the more tools and tactics you can deploy to make it a reality.

_____

_____

_____

_____

_____

_____

_____

_____

_____

_____

Instead of just passing time or mindlessly responding to other people's wants and needs, you'll have a vision for how to navigate your day the way you want, in a way that's meaningful and energizing for you. Furthermore, the more clarity you have on how your perfect day looks, the more likely you can create goals that will take you to that vision, which is exactly what we'll do now.

Chapter Seven

Vision Lights, Goals Define

> "When you have the right purpose, you'll easily develop the right vision. When you have the right vision, you'll quickly recognize the right goal."
>
> — Bob Proctor, Purpose, Vision, Goals

It was Christmas break, and I impatiently waited while my grandfather's computer connected to the Internet via dial-up modem in the basement of their split-level 1960's era house. My heart was racing, and the connection to Purdue University's grading website was taking longer than it takes to boil a block of dry ice.

I only wanted to see one grade. Linear Algebra. The rest of the classes I took that semester didn't matter. I knew I had done well. Or at least, well enough to pass. But Linear Algebra was a different beast. Going into the final exam, my grade was a solid F. I was about to see if I had raised it enough to pass.

When the page finally loaded, I took it all in, exploded from my chair, and ran upstairs. The adults were drinking coffee and having a serious conversation, which I interrupted by shouting, "I got a D!"

Their silence was deafening, confusion scribbled all over their faces. So, I clarified, "I got a D in Linear Algebra!"

It didn't help. Getting a D in my house was never celebrated, so my excitement over a shitty grade didn't make sense. I tried one more time. "I passed! I passed Linear Algebra!" To which they smiled politely, muttered an unconvincing affirmation that sounded something like "good job," and went back to their chat. I realized only later that they didn't appreciate my excitement in the least.

My purpose was to build a career in technology. To do that, my vision was to be a computer science graduate from Purdue University. Passing Linear Algebra was simply a goal along the way. Not getting an A+ in Linear Algebra. Not even getting a B or C. I just wanted to pass. If I passed, I would move one step closer to my vision. If I failed, I would be set back a whole semester.

It's easy to get purpose, vision, and goals confused. Though related, they are very different animals. As we discussed, purpose is the north star that guides your every move. It's your way forward, the thing you were put on this earth to do, your reason for being. Vision, on the other hand, is the outline for how you will live each day as you move toward your purpose. It guides you on who on you want to be while heading toward that light. Goals are the checkpoints along the way. They are the future achievements you can measure. They indicate whether you are on the right track.

The course you chart will not likely be a calm one. It may twist and wind through dense fog, obscuring your north star from view. Goals are like buoys: close enough that you can see and navigate to the next one, and the one after that, and the one after that, until you finally achieve all that you set out to.

For all the reasons we discussed in the last chapter, purpose isn't enough. And, as we'll see in this chapter, vision isn't enough either. Knowing who you want to be, knowing how you want to live, and knowing what kind of person you want to become are important, but if you don't actually put in the effort to get there, you'll still be dreaming about these ideas 20 years from now. You'll have a grand vision for your life, but won't actually live it, experience the failures and successes along the way, or ever enjoy the results of it. Hence the need for goals.

If purpose is your *why* and vision is your how, goals are your *what*. They are the third and last ring in Simon Sinek's target, surrounding your vision (how), which in turn is surrounding your purpose (why). Goals are the navigation points along your lifelong path, helping you build momentum and telling you if you're on the right course (or not). They assure you, even if the clouds are so thick you can't see where you're going, that you've sailed in the right direction. And, once you make it to one goal, it becomes easier to see the next.

Of course, this assumes you've created a good goal. A goal that doesn't have a set due date isn't a good goal. Similarly, a goal whose due date is so far in the future you'll face no challenge meeting it is also not a good goal. You've only got so much time before the wind runs out of your sails. If it's going to take you a lifetime to meet your first goal, you'll never reach your North Star. So, we need to create goals that challenge you, motivate you, and help you track progress along the way. There are many ways to do this, but only one way is the SMART way.

Defining a Goal

If a goal without a due date isn't a good goal, what is then? Simple. A goal that has five specific characteristics: specificity, measurability, achievability, relevancy, and timeliness. If you have a Specific, Measurable, Achievable, Relevant, Time-bound goal, you have a SMART goal.

The SMART goal-setting system has been covered ad nauseam by hundreds of business bloggers on the Internet, but we're not using it (only) for business here, we're using it for life. So, let's review each of these five parts of a goal in the context of setting goals that align with our vision and purpose.

A Good Goal Is Specific

A goal that isn't specific doesn't clearly tell you what you're trying to accomplish. "Drive west" isn't a good goal. It raises all kinds of questions. Where west? For how long? When do you need to get to where you're going?

A few years ago, while running a sales organization for a microelectronics company, I set a goal of making somewhere between $1.5 and $3 million in bookings that year. That's not specific, that's a range. At the beginning of the year, I had aspirations of making the achieving the upper end of that goal. When times got tough, I started looking for excuses to achieve the lower end. Throughout the year, I found it hard to focus on relevant tasks necessary to achieve this goal. The result? I didn't fall anywhere in the range. I fell far short of even the low end.

Getting specific with your goals means using words like *must, will,* or *shall.*

- I *shall* book $3 million in revenue by the end of the year is better than I'll *try* to book $3 million in revenue by the end of the year.

- I *must* make two sales this month is better than I'll *attempt* to make two sales this month.

- I *shall* weigh 215 pounds with 15% body fat by September 31st is better than *lose weight.*

When goals aren't specific, it leaves open the question, "what am I trying to achieve here?" Make your goals as specific as possible so there's no doubt in your mind what you're trying to achieve and when you've actually achieved it.

A Good Goal is Measurable

If you want to get something done, you have to track it. And, if you want to track something, you need to be able to measure it. If you can't measure your goal, it's not a goal. It's a wish. A measurable goal speaks to you. It tells you when it's done. A measurable goal alerts you if you are on track along the way.

Goals with numbers are easy to measure. If you must book $3 million by the end of the year, then it's easy to measure when you'll be done. It's also easy to measure along the way. By the end of June, you should have $1.5 million booked. By the end of January, you should have $250,000 booked. A measurable goal like this can even be tracked daily—$3 million divided by 365 makes for a goal of $8,219.18 per day.

Of course, goals rarely track this closely to plan. But being able to measure how far off you are to your goal will help you know how to adjust. If you're halfway through the year and have achieved only 10% of your target, it's clear your strategy isn't working and you'll need to find a different way to a) achieve your original goal, and b) make up 40% to stay on track.

When goals aren't measurable, it's hard to know when you're done, and impossible to know whether you'll finish. Make your goals measurable, so there's no doubt in your mind if and when you'll achieve them.

A Good Goal is Achievable

The hardest part of goal setting is finding the balance between a goal set too low vs. too high. Too often, people set goals that are lofty and unachievable. Just as often, they set goals that are downright impossible. While you may want to make $100 million this year, if you only made $1 million last year while working 80 hours a week, it's not likely to happen. Instead of setting a 10,000% increase over last year's achievements, set a reasonable goal of $1.2 million (a 20% increase over last year's goal). A good goal is challenging but attainable.

Furthermore, goals should be within your lane to accomplish. A goal isn't achievable if you don't have the resources, responsibility, or authority to make it happen. If you have a goal of booking $1.2 million in new business but have moved into a role that's no longer responsible for sales, then achieving that goal is completely out of your control.

In Steven Covey's popular self-help book, 7 Habits of Highly Effective People, he discusses the differences between our "circle of influence" and "circle of concern."

The circle of concern is filled with issues and matters we care about. Things like our health, our children, getting to work on time, political issues, polar bears in Antarctica, and how many people have tested positive worldwide during a global pandemic. Some of the things we have control over. Most, we don't.

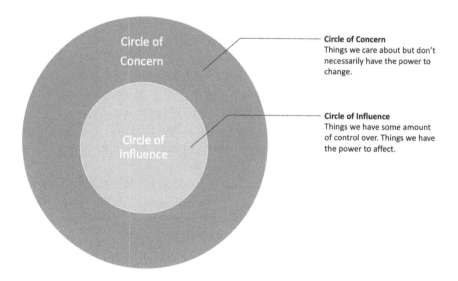

Circle of Concern
Things we care about but don't necessarily have the power to change.

Circle of Influence
Things we have some amount of control over. Things we have the power to affect.

Contrast that with the circle of influence, which is filled with issues that we have some ability to change or affect. Things like our health—which we can affect (either positively or negatively) through eating, exercise, and stress—fall in our circle of influence. Our goals should fall in this circle.

Goals that are not achievable are not good goals. Make sure the goals you set are possible to accomplish, within your scope of work, and within your circle of influence so that you can directly impact their outcome and have a shot at attaining them.

A Good Goal is Relevant

A relevant goal is one that improves some aspect of your life or business. Just last year, I set a goal to meditate for 30 minutes daily. All the cool podcasters were blathering on about how the most successful people in the world meditate. I wanted to jump on the bandwagon and realize the benefits they were talking about.

My goal was achievable, measurable, and specific. But as I would soon find out, my goal wasn't relevant. Other activities in my day, like journaling, took the place of meditation. Benefits such as mental clarity and reduced stress, while scientifically proven, felt distant and vague. Meditation was consuming 30 minutes of my morning, time that I'd have otherwise spent on something that actually helped me achieve my goals. After a few months, I dropped the daily practice, killed the goal, and replaced it with a more relevant one—planning daily.

Meditation wasn't really *my* goal. It was the goal of podcasters and Internet influencers pushing their own agenda. Doing what they were simply didn't help.

A good goal is relevant. It improves some aspect of your life or business. And, by keeping your goals relevant, you'll work towards your vision and purpose instead of away from them.

A Good Goal is Time-Bound

You probably noticed end-dates in the goals above. The goal for $3 million was set for "the end of the year." The goal for body weight and fat percentage was "by September 31st." Even the irrelevant goal of meditating was time-bound, as it was set to happen "30 minutes daily." If I didn't rake in $3 million by the end of the year, I would know that I hadn't achieved my goal. If I hadn't weighed 215 with 15% body fat by September 31st, my goal had failed. If I didn't meditate for 30 minutes that day, I couldn't check off that goal as a success.

Goals that aren't time-bound will limp along forever, never pushing you to achieve. It won't be clear when you're supposed to be done, so you'll have no incentive to work on them in the face of other urgent matters. Make sure you set time constraints for your goals, so you know not only what you need to accomplish but by when.

That's the SMART Goal Setting System

We're about to write out goals that align with your vision and purpose. For each one, use the SMART system to ensure your goal is specific, measurable, achievable, relevant, and time bound. In fact, as you write any goal, ask yourself these five questions:

1. Is my goal **specific** enough that I know exactly what needs to be done?

2. Can my goal be **measured** at any point along the way to its completion?

3. Do I have the authority, responsibility, and resources to **achieve** my goal?

4. Is my goal **relevant** such that it will help me achieve a bigger goal, my vision, or my purpose?

5. Do I know exactly what **time** my goal is done, either successfully accomplished or failed?

Setting Goals for Your Vision and Purpose

We set goals to help us achieve our vision and purpose. We set goals so we can work on, stay focused on, and get clear on what matters. And, what matters to you will stem from those seven important areas in your life, which you've already defined in your vision and purpose.

So, for each area, create a specific, measurable, achievable, relevant, and time-bound goals such that, when you achieve it, you'll be one step closer to achieving your vision and living your purpose.

Some goals will be easy to set, like the $3 million bookings target for me. That goal was SMART in every way, and it needed to be done. It aligned perfectly with our company vision and purpose. It also aligned with my vision for Wealth and Finances.

Other goals, like relationship goals, are challenging. Building a relationship between my children and I is not as easy to define as a sales target. Do I measure when they listen, help around the house, show love towards each other, or respect to my wife and me? Whereas sales goals are cut and dried, relationship goals are more touchy-feely, more human. But they can be set. Just because they're touch-feely doesn't mean they have to be left to chance.

> "Everything that's important to you in life can be measured. You just have to find something to measure that drives the behavior you desire."
>
> — Elaine Mehlberg MS CCC SLP, Speech Pathologist, Capital Speech Therapy

You can measure anything. You can create goals for anything. The number of times I reward my children for a good deed could be one measurement. The amount of time I spend with each child one-on-one could be another. Those measurements can turn a goal into something that can be tracked outside of your gut.

Whatever your goals, take care not to set them too close or too far into the future. It may be clear to you what matters today, but one year from now is far off. A lot can happen between now and then, events that could drastically change what matters in your life. If it feels right to set your goals one year out, do so. If that's too long, try three months. If that still feels too long, set your goals one month out, but no closer. Less than one month doesn't give you much time to accomplish anything significant. Anything more than a year and it becomes too easy to over or underestimate how much you can get done.

Your Health and Fitness Goals

_____

_____

_____

Your Friends and Family Goals

_____

_____

_____

Your Wealth and Finances Goals

_____

_____

_____

Your Spiritual and Self Goals

_____

_____

_____

Your Career and Business Goals

_____

_____

_____

Your Hobbies and Side-Hustles Goals

_____

_____

_____

Your Attitude and Character Goals

_____

_____

_____

What are your goals? How will they align with your vision and purpose? Are they specific, measurable, achievable, relevant, and time-bound? If you've written them down in the spaces above and can answer these questions, you are ready to break down your goals into small increments so that there are no surprises along the way. Which is precisely what we'll do in Part III.

PART III

Plan, Schedule, Track

How to get from where you are to where you want to be

"When [life] is wasted in heedless luxury and spent on no good activity, we are forced at last by death's final constraint to realize that it has passed away before we knew it was passing." — Seneca

^ Translation: Time flies. Use it wisely or die with regret.

Chapter Eight

Laying the Groundwork

"A goal without a plan is just a wish." — Antoine de Saint-Exupéry

It's January 3rd, my first day back from holiday vacation, and my boss just handed me a $1.5 million dollar sales goal.

I didn't choose this goal. I didn't even have a say in it. If I had, I would have chosen a modest $500,000. But no, this $1.5 million target was calculated for me and stapled to my resume. Hit my target, and I'd keep my job to enjoy an even bigger sales target next year. Miss, and I'd hit the streets.

When a number that large is sitting in front of you, success feels insurmountable. I could imagine a mountain of pennies adding up to 1.5 million dollars, crushing the life out of me, laughing at my (mis)fortune.

With that kind of money as my goal, the pressure to perform was high. I couldn't deal with it by wishing and hoping for success. One year was too far away, and I could easily get off track a few weeks in, not know it, and have no way to catch up—I couldn't magically make up a $1.5 million deficit in the final weeks of the year.

Don't get me wrong, I love a big, hairy, audacious goal. Setting one will kickstart you into action. But, if it's so big and far out you can't actually achieve something soon, you'll lose interest quickly. Hence the need to create smaller, bite sized, manageable milestones along the way.

Reaching a small, achievable milestone on the path to a bigger goal gives you a sense of accomplishment before the excitement of getting started wears off. Reach another milestone, you'll feel that excitement again. This excitement builds momentum. It changes your expectations for what's possible. You'll no longer be satisfied living someone else's goals and dreams. You'll turn into a goal monster, setting bigger and better targets for yourself, increasing your confidence, and building more momentum over time.

Break down your goal into small milestones, achieve your milestones, feel great before the excitement wears off. Rinse and repeat.

Breaking Down Your Goals

Breaking down a sales goal is simple math. Take my $1.5 million sales target, for example. $1.5 million divided by 12 months is $125,000 per month. Divide that same number by 52 weeks and you come up with about $28,846 per week. Divide that number yet again by 365 days and you arrive at just over $4,109 per day.

What once seemed like a mountain to scale now looks more like a staircase where each step, which can be taken one at a time, moves you closer to the top. More so, this breakdown gives you the information necessary to know where you stand throughout the year—You'll see if you are getting off track and, if so, by how far.

In an ideal world, tracking your goal would map perfectly to real life. Starting January 1st with a goal of zero, you would sell exactly $4,109 daily and $125,000 monthly. In an ideal world, you'd get to the end of the year and have drawn a straight line from $0 to your $1.5M sales target, which might look something like this:

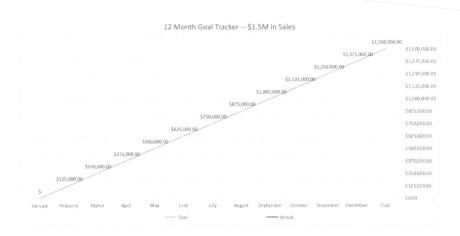

But the real world is not ideal. Many factors will influence your ability to keep pace perfectly with your goal throughout the year. Some weeks will be great. Some will be slow. Some weeks you'll crush it. Other weeks won't bring any gains. Because of this, your tracking may look more like this:

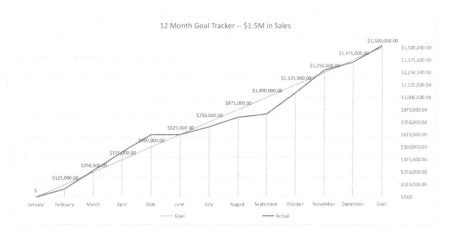

A little ugly, but that's okay. The purpose of tracking your goals isn't to beat yourself up at the end of each day but rather to evaluate whether you need to change. As this chart shows, sales get sluggish in September. The trajectory toward the end of the year is worrisome, and you'll need to find a way to increase sales. On the flip side, when sales are hot in May, you could spend some time focusing on other important goals you have for other areas of your life (more on this later).

This applies beyond sales. Weight-loss, meditation, or any other types of goals will run into issues. Unforeseen circumstances will undoubtedly prevent you from staying perfectly on track. To prevent that from happening, we can move from measuring our goals after the fact to beforehand. This entails finding those underlying drivers that will get you to your goal—finding the fundamental things you must do on a daily, weekly, monthly basis to make an impact—better known as finding your lead measures.

Determine Your Lead Measures

In the Four Disciplines of Execution, Chris McChesney, Sean Covey, and Jim Huling outline the differences between lag measures and lead measures. Normal goals are usually classified as lag measures. That's because the information necessary to know whether you've achieved the goal *lags* the goal itself. For example, I wouldn't know if my $1.5 million sales goal was successful until the clock struck midnight at the end of the year. This is problematic for a number of reasons, not the least of which is that it's difficult, if not impossible, to stay in control.

Transforming your goals into *lead* measures, measurements you can take *before* the goal date hits, takes back that control. Over time, the accumulation of many small lead measures will result in completing your longer-term goal.

During high school, my favorite outdoor hobby target shooting with bow and arrow. I'd stand in my backyard and fire arrows into a bale of hay from 20 yards away. With practice, I could consistently hit a quarter-sized target, but only if my lead measures were in place. Without my lead measures, I'd miss. Often by a lot.

Measuring where my arrow landed was a lag measure. If my arrow hit the quarter-sized center, I'd consider it a success. If it didn't, I'd try again. This measurement was helpful to making adjustments *after* shooting, but utterly useless for changing the outcome prior. To consistently hit the center, I needed lead measures, things I could measure *before* releasing my arrow.

One lead measure was drawing my arrow and bowstring back the exact same distance every time. I'd also check that my left arm was straight, elbow locked. I'd wrap my right index finger around the string and pull it back to touch the right corner of my lips. Fingers finally situated, I'd rest the bowstring above my fingers gently on the tip of my nose.

With these lead measures in place, I was set for the perfect shot. I'd look "through" the string, down the arrow shaft, towards the target and release my arrow to its destination, dead center. If any of these lead measures weren't in place, there was no telling where my arrow would go.

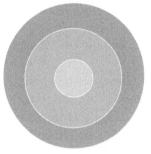

Lead Measures
1. Measure the wind
2. Measure the distance
3. Measure the aim

Increase chances of hitting...
Completely in your control...

Lag Measures
Hit or miss?
Nothing I can do now...

Back to my $1.5 million sales goal, while it was helpful to break down that goal into smaller daily goals, each was still a lag measure; I wouldn't know whether I'd hit my daily goal until the end of the day. To transform that lag measure into a lead measure, I needed to understand the smallest increment of work I could perform that would result in a sale. If, for example, I was selling a product that was, on average, $250,000, I knew I would need to sell six to achieve my target. I knew from experience that, in order to sell one product, I'd need to host five meetings. And I estimated that, in order to get one customer meeting, I would have to call around thirteen people in my market. That's thirteen people times five meetings times six products in a year, or 390 people. That's 33 people per month (rounded up), eight people per week (rounded up), or two new customer calls every day.

While I should still track daily progress toward my $1.5 million goal with the lag measure of $4,109 per day, tracking how many people I called per day was completely and easily in my control. Probabilistically, calling this many people would land me enough business to meet or exceed my overarching goal.

How do I bring in $1.5 million? Make sales.

How do I make sales? Pitch prospects.

How do I pitch prospects? Make calls.

How do I make calls? Just fucking do it.

Making calls is therefore my lead measure.

Science shows that setting a goal makes it far more likely to achieve it. But you can go further by breaking down your goals. Doing so will give you a better understanding of how you'll achieve that goal and whether you're on track along the way. Go further yet by creating lead measures—daily activities that will add up to goal achievement—and you'll have aligned your actions with your goals. The result? You'll be far more likely to get done what you want to get done by the end of the year. So long as you plan for failure.

Planning for Failure

An obstacle, no matter how trivial, can be devastating to your progress, sometimes killing it completely. What will you do when one gets between you and your goals? Because, it will. And, without an answer to that question in advance, it'll be too easy to turn around at the first sign of trouble and end up right where you started.

That's because, when you set an expectation that isn't met, your brain withholds dopamine, which can put you into a severe funk. This can last for days, destroying your progress and possibly halting any momentum you've created to date. To prevent that, let's plan for failure by clearing a path to your goals. It's as easy to do as creating a list of risks and obstacles.

Write down anything you can think of that would get in your way. Write down any*one* you can think of that would benefit from you failing. Write down all the reasons you might find to slow down, quit, or have doubt in your work. Then, for each one, write down an action plan to prevent it from happening in the first place or killing it when it does.

Obstacle   How Will I Prevent or Clear This Obstacle?

_____

_____

_____

_____

_____

Unexpected roadblocks will pop up. No question. But if you've planned for failure, you'll have anticipated issues that could destroy your momentum and put you in a dopamine-deprived funk. You'll be ready to break through those roadblocks instead of going into panic mode, stalling out, or stopping progress for good.

Chapter Nine

Habits and Skills

> "We become what we repeatedly do."
>
> — Sean Covey, The 7 Habits of Highly Effective Teens

Not every goal can be divided into predictable chunks. Some, like learning a new language, will take an unknown amount of time and require consistent, daily practice.

Fitness goals can be tracked by measuring attributes like weight or body fat but are just as difficult to predict and require consistent effort. Even a well-defined project like the one I'm embarked on now—writing a book—pushes me to become a better writer, a lifelong endeavor that demands persistent growth. *Learn a new language* or *get fit* or *write better* are not good goals. They are too vague, and too hard to track. But where traditional goals fail, habits can pick up the slack.

Instead of setting a goal to be fluent in Spanish by Christmas (which is impossible to predict), you could create a habit of studying Spanish for 30 minutes daily. Instead of setting a goal to lose 15 pounds in three months (which says nothing about how you would get

85

there), you could create a habit of exercising 30 minutes every day. Instead of setting a goal to become a recognized writer by the end of the year (which is influenced by factors out of your control), you could set a habit of writing daily for one hour before going to bed.

Habits, like goals, are either done or not done. But unlike goals, the strength of a habit comes in its consistent, frequent, and recurring practice. Habits are predictable, action oriented, and in your control. They build you into a version of yourself that doesn't currently exist— a version that can help you reach your goals, achieve your vision, and live your purpose.

My first habit tracker was Coach.me, a simple iPhone app that reminded me to perform customizable habits. Every day I woke up early, meditated, flossed my teeth, exercised, ate healthy, and followed a few other "good habits," I would check the box. It was highly effective. After a few months of tracking my daily flossing, I found myself doing it without thinking. After waking early a few months in a row, I rose before sunrise with or without the app.

Studies have shown that it takes 66 days to build a habit (Clear, n.d.). Once built, it becomes engrained into our being. Our brain runs on autopilot and we no longer have to think about what we're doing. We no longer spend energy considering how or when. We reduce decision fatigue, like Steve Jobs who wore the same blue jeans and black turtleneck every damn day. By filtering our habits through the lens of our purpose, vision, and goals, we can build autopilot functions for things that matter in our life saving valuable energy, time, and increasing the likelihood of success.

How to Build Good Habits

Like goals, habits can be good and bad. Flossing your teeth? Good. Biting your nails? Bad. Certain habits help you achieve your goals, others distract you from them. Unfortunately, a balance of good and bad habits is not productive. For all the good habits instilled in your life, one bad habit can undo all your progress.

Habits like biting your nails aren't significant. They won't detract from work that matters in any meaningful way. Others, however, can be crushing. Reading frivolous articles on the Internet may destroy the time you would otherwise have to work on what matters. Watching three hours of Netflix and stuffing Peanut M&Ms mindlessly into your mouth every night would undo any and all progress made exercising earlier in the day. Which is why, ridding yourself of bad habits is the first thing you must focus on.

What bad habits are holding you back from these goals? To identify them, think through a normal workday. Think about every detail, from the moment you wake up until the moment your head hits the pillow at night. Think about what time you get up, when you shower, when you brush your teeth, and how long you spend doing each. Do you use your phone, how long do you stare at your closet picking out the right clothing, how long do you stare into the refrigerator picking your breakfast? Every detail matters. Because, these details are the ones you face over and over, every day of your life. Some habits will be useful to your end goal. Others you'll notice are wasteful.

Once you have your list, choose the most destructive habit to your goals. If that's watching three hours of Netflix and eating Peanut M&Ms at night before bed, great. If it's spending too much time staring into the refrigerator deciding what to eat for breakfast, perfect. I'm guilty of both. Just choose your worst. And, keep in mind, your bad habit doesn't have to be time-based. Checking social media while brushing your teeth in the morning arguably doesn't take any time out of your day, but if it puts you in a bad, passive, or otherwise negative mindset, it's not worth doing and should be replaced.

Whatever your worst habit is, this is our target. We're aiming to tie an anchor to its feet and throw it overboard. Unfortunately, unlike a bad meeting on your calendar, you won't simply be able to delete it and get your time back. Habits don't work that way. Habits must be replaced, lest you return to your old ways with nothing changed.

"A nail is driven out by another nail; habit is overcome by habit."

— Erasmus

In order to replace a habit, we must identify our triggers. Besides Netflix and peanut M&M binging, my next worst habit was checking email, news, and social media first thing in the morning. It distracted from my vision and goals. Each one was an administrative activity that could wait until more urgent matters were complete. Checking email, news, and social media easily consumed 30 minutes of my morning. If work was slow, I could happily spend an hour or more sifting through one notification after another. It was simple, braindead work. I gravitated to it.

As I'd come to realize, my phone was the trigger. Specifically, looking at my phone while brewing coffee. Though coffee took only two or three minutes to brew, it was enough time to get entrenched in the notifications that had trickled in overnight. Social media and news headlines had me hooked, hard, and I'd relentlessly scroll through juicy headlines, funny videos, or insightful memes in search of another dopamine hit.

With my trigger identified, I was able to replace my bad habit with a good one at exactly the right moment; the moment after I turn on the coffee pot, right before getting lost in a world of headlines and social media. Instead of pulling out my phone, I would do something that helped fulfill my vision and goals. In my case, that was writing a minimum of 1,000 words in this very book.

Now, instead of getting lost in notifications, I would open up my laptop (on which I'd have my writing program open and ready to roll) and start writing while the coffee brewed. My bad habit trigger, my phone, would stay out of arms reach so I couldn't pick it up and destroy my morning.

Here's what a bad habit replacement sequence might look like for you:

1. Identify bad habit — For me, surfing news and social media first thing in the morning. What's the most damaging habit to your time?

2. Identify bad habit trigger — For me, starting to browse news and social media when my coffee is brewing. What is the one thing, the one moment when your bad habit begins?

3. Identify good habit — For me, writing 1,000 words per day toward this book. What's a simple yet effective good habit that can replace a bad one?

4. Begin work on your good habit right before your bad habit is triggered — For me, before pouring water in the coffee pot to

get it brewing, open my laptop to my writing app. How can you put your good habit into action the moment the old, bad habit is triggered?

As you seek to replace your bad habit trigger, choose a low-hanging fruit. Something that will make a massive difference to your goals but isn't terribly hard to accomplish. For my goal of publishing a book, writing 1,000 words per day didn't take long and would put me on track to finishing a draft within three months.

This sequence of replacing bad habits with good ones will take discipline but is dead simple to follow. And, once a bad habit is eradicated, you can move on to the next bad habit that's distracting you from achieving all that you want to achieve. After doing this repeatedly, and for as long as it takes to establish new, good habits, your new trigger will be carved in stone. You'll kick off your new habits automatically, without thinking, which will support your goals, which will support your vision, which will support your purpose.

Building Skills

Think about your goals and ask yourself if you already have the skills necessary to achieve them. If your goals are challenging enough, the answer is likely "no."

After all, if you knew how to make a million dollars, you'd already be a millionaire. If you knew how to pack on 12 pounds of muscle in 12 months, you'd already be fit as a show horse. Whatever your goal, if you already knew how to do it, you'd already have completed it. But if you don't, that's okay. It simply means you'll need to acquire new skills to get there.

In my example above, writing 1,000 words per day was a useful habit that would help me achieve a goal of drafting this book in three months. But if I didn't get better at writing, those 1,000 words would suck. So, I set a skill to read well-written books, studying how the author conveyed meaning. I read books about writing to learn the tools good writers use; tools like grammar and structure and storytelling. I even hired a coach to tell me where and how I could make my writing better. I'm no Henry David Thoreau, but hopefully these pages are at least bearable.

Skills, like making money, getting fit, parenting, or anything else worth doing, require continual learning. Once you've defined your purpose, your vision, your goals, and your habits, defining what skills you need for your journey is the final step before planning how to get it all done (something we'll do in Chapter Eleven).

What could you learn to make achieving your goals easier? What books you could study, what videos could you watch, what research could you read, what articles could you review, what mentors could you hire to your goals possible?

#

Until now, we've identified our zenith for every important area of our life. We've imagined a better future. We've identified habits and skills that will help us achieve our goals. We've even broken down our goals into measurable milestones so we can track progress along the way. But if we keep on standing here on this old world of chaos and disorganization, we will never reach that new world of balance, productivity, and achievement.

So now it's time to learn how to set aside time to do the work. It's time to learn how to track achievements and milestones over time. It's time to look at the last part of your system, the part where you take your purpose, vision, goals, habits, and skills, and draw up a detailed plan you'll follow to get the work done and reach your destination.

Bill Burnett once said, "You can imagine a career and a life that don't exist; you can build that future you, and as a result your life will change." I like this quote, but it's missing something. Just imagining a career won't allow you to build a future and get results. You actually have to put in the work.

Chapter Ten

Designing Your Life

> "Lead a life of your own design, on your own terms. Not one that others or the environment have scripted for you."
>
> — Tony Robbins

Early in my career, at our rag-tag startup out of Indiana, our leadership team kicked off an exciting new project and assigned me to the team. We'd have two years to design, develop, and ship a new web tool that (we hoped) would make us millions. So naturally, as a trained software engineer, I got right to work coding. When our VP of Engineering found out I had immediately started work, he walked into my office and threatened to take my keyboard and monitor away. I thought he was joking. He was dead serious.

Experience told him that developing software without a design was perilous. If we didn't stop and plan out the next two years, our project would fall into disarray and we'd be forced to spend considerable time redesigning it from scratch. And so, under threat of losing our computers, we gathered our team and sat around a whiteboard to discuss exactly what needed to happen, when, and who would do the work. We finished the project, two years later, on time and on budget.

Our VP of Engineering knew that if we didn't design our software first, it would design itself — and that design wouldn't be pretty, let alone usable. He knew that, if we didn't plan our time, we'd fall victim to constant distraction. Little things like checking emails, holding meetings, and chats at the water cooler would add up, and we'd fall behind on our tasks. Worse, without a design and plan to follow, we wouldn't know we were behind until it was too late. And, once lost at sea, we'd never find our way back. We'd wander from island to island, searching for our destination while bumping into each other, getting frustrated, and never knowing the right path.

The answer, as he taught us, is to plan. It's to align the work we'll need to do throughout the year with our purpose, vision, and goals. For software development, that meant architecture diagrams, flow charts, and project plans. For you, it means planning where you want to be, what you want to get done, and what would make for a successful year. It means laying out your upcoming month, week, and day.

This part of the process is no joke. Especially the yearly planning. It takes time and thought. If you're not serious about getting productive and finding time for your friends and family, then now is the time to find another book to read. But if you are, I can promise you this: When you're done, you'll know *exactly* what you need to do tomorrow to achieve your broken-down goals for the week. You'll know *exactly* what you need to do next week to achieve your objectives for the month. And you'll know *exactly* what you need to do this month to end up, 365 days from now, with your feet up on the couch, watching your favorite movie with a loved one, drinking an expensive bottle of wine in celebration of an amazingly successful year.

Start by Planning Your Year

Don't get caught up thinking you need to plan your year on January 1st. I don't care if it's Septembriary 72nd, if you don't have a plan for the remainder of your year, you don't have a plan. And if you don't have a plan, you're just *hoping* for the future you want instead building a path to the vision and purpose you've now designed.

Every year, whenever that may be, we're going to plan out your year. If it your first time and it's the middle of the year, make your plan for the remainder of the year. Next time around, start this yearly planning process on December 31st.

Importantly, we're not going to just think about it. We're going to write it down. You already have many pieces of this puzzle complete; your purpose statement, your vision statement, your personal and business and family and other goals. And, you've broken these goals down into smaller, measurable chunks. You've even spent some time looking at how to clear a path to these goals and translate them into lead measures. Now let's put it all together into a plan for your year.

Your yearly plan is going to be organized into multiple sections, each section guiding you closer to a structure that you can use to plan your months, weeks, and days.

1. Goals Aligned with Purpose

2. Thinking Big

3. What Matters Most

4. Looking Back from the Future

5. Long-Term Vision and Plan to Get There

6. Skills You Need

Let's build each section independently using the guidelines below.

Goals Aligned with Purpose

Do you remember these important life areas? Check out the graphic for a reminder. Now, for this section of your yearly plan, you will align your purpose with your goals. For each life area, write just one or two sentences stating what your goal is and how it aligns with your purpose.

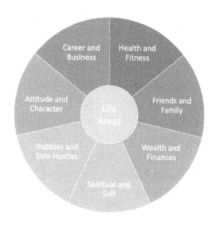

For example, my Career and Business goals this year is to get revenue. Based on my commission plan, I want to sell $3.33 million worth of product. So, I wrote this:

> **Career and Business:** Get revenue. $3.33 million dollars' worth to be exact. Why? Because I need to sell $3.33M worth of product to meet my financial goals based on my commission plan.

With all my major goals for the Career and Business area of my life listed (in my case, only one) and my *why* for each goal written, I could move onto the other six important life areas. Each one should have their own goals as you've created from Chapter Seven. Write those goals here, and then write down why each one is important to you. Here's what the rest of mine looked like:

> **Hobbies and Side Hustle:** My goal for my website, www.moderndavinci.net was always to get more subscribers. But do I need Modern da Vinci anymore? I'm thinking a www.michaelmehlberg.com website would be more powerful. More connected to my book (Home Early). More connected to my thoughts. More connected to the message I want to convey. More connected with Medium where I can make money with my writing. With www.michaelmehlberg.com, I can connect with my subscribers better, which in turn just may get more of them. For all these reasons, I need to get www.michaelmehlberg.com up and running ASAP.
>
> Beyond my website though, I need my book to connect with people. That means publishing it. That means writing the hell out of it. That means connecting it to my Medium and website and social media and marketing efforts.
>
> **Friends a Family:** Connect with my children and wife and dog. Be there with them and for them. Put the phone and computer away when I'm not working and really spend time with them. Play games. Help cook dinner. Take them to the park. Go on bike-rides and walks and talk with them. Why? Because they are what matters most. They are the reason I work all day and push a side-hustle at night. So when I'm with them, be with them. They matter most. Make sure they know it.

Spiritual and Self: I want to read topics that inspire me and let those topics inspire my passion and purpose (writing). For my spirituality, I want to connect with the message of the church. I want to understand the church and its teachings in my life.

Health and Fitness: Connect my mind and my body. Connect it in the gym, while working out, feeling the mind/muscle connection grow my strength. Connect my nutrition with my goals, eating that which helps me accomplish them. Why? Because I've just been going through the motions this last half of this last year. My growth, or lack thereof, is evident. It's time to really map what I want to do with what I'm actually doing.

I left out *Wealth and Finance* and *Attitude and Character*. They are too personal to me, and you get the idea. Begin planning your own year by writing down each goal for each major area of your life, then writing why that goal is important. It may not seem worthwhile now, but in a month or two when the excitement of planning your year has worn off, reviewing these goals and purpose for each will re-inspire you to keep going strong.

Thinking Big

Now, for each of the seven areas, I want you to write down your biggest goal for the year. What is the one big thing that, if you could get it done this year, would make for an awesome year. If it doesn't seem that big, think bigger and write it down.

> "Thinking big is essential to extraordinary results... the only actions that become springboards to succeeding big are those informed by big thinking to begin with."
>
> — Gary Keller, The One Thing

If you're struggling with this one, write down five big goals that you want to accomplish in the upcoming year. Then, cross off the bottom four. The one remaining is your one big thing that would make for an incredible year.

Big Goal #1

_____

_____

_____

Big Goal #2

_____

_____

_____

Big Goal #3

_____

_____

_____

Big Goal #4

_____

_____

_____

Big Goal #5

_____

Most Important Goal?

Here's what mine looks like. Nothing complicated. Just a few words describing what my big idea is for having an amazing year:

Career and Business — $3.33M in Sales

Hobbies and Side Hustle — Convert website to www.michaelmehlberg.com, Publish Home Early, First Draft of New Book

Friends and Family — Create an amazing year for my family with trips, connecting, and making memories.
Health and Fitness — Pyramid physique

Attitude and Character — Stillness, calm, collected, confident.

Spiritual and Self — Connected

What Matters Most

Some things matter most. Others do not. As we discussed in the last section, *Clearing a Path to Our Goals*, those things that do not matter can be distractions for the things that do. In this section, and for each area of your life, list anything that comes to mind that is distracting your from working on what matters.

Many times, those distractions are us struggling to keep everything in balance. The secret is that not everything needs to be in balance. In fact, some things need to get extremely out of balance so that we have the time to focus on what matters. What do you need to let fall out of balance to be able to work on that which matters?

"To achieve extraordinary results you must choose what matters most and give it all the time it demands. This requires getting extremely out of balance in relation to all other work issues."

— Ayodeji Awosika

Here are some things that are distracting from my main goals:

_____

_____

_____

_____

_____

Next, list one thing you can do that will make everything else easier or unnecessary. You can organize this by goal or by each of the seven life areas, or both. The point here is to find that most important activity that will give you the biggest return on investment.

"Don't focus on being busy; focus on being productive. Allow what matters most to drive your day. Once you've figured out what actually matters, keep asking what matters most until there is only one thing left. That core activity goes at the top of your success list."

— Gary Keller, Jay Papasan, The One Thing

What's the Most Value Creating Activity You Can Do for Each Area of Your Life?

Career and Business

_____

Hobbies and Side Hustles

_____

Friends and Family

_____

Health and Fitness

_____

Attitude and Character

_____

Wealth and Finance

_____

Spiritual and Self

_____

Finally, working on what matters most sometimes means getting help from others. You don't have to do everything yourself. What role models can you look to that have done what you want to do before? What training can you take that will help you get to your goals faster? Who could be your mentor to teach you all the ways of your future? List them. Either for each life area, or for each goal, or both.

Don't forget, if I haven't done something before, look for role models or others that have accomplished what I've accomplished and learn from them so I can accomplish myself.

Who are some role models and I can look to to help?

_____

_____

_____

Looking Back from the Future

Finally, paste your one-year vision statement here. If you've already created a one-year vision from Chapter Six, there's no need to recreate it or modify it. Just use what you have. If you're vision is more generic, use the questions outlined in that chapter to draft a one-year vision, looking back from the future. Imagine yourself a year from now and all that you've accomplished. Describe how amazing this year has been and why. You'll review this monthly to a) see if you want to modify it and b) remind yourself of this vision so it's always top of mind in everything you do.

Vision

_____

_____

_____

_____

_____

_____

_____

Long-Term Vision and Plan to Get There

Your vision statement above is a thorough account of your year, looking back one-year from the future. In this section, I want you to write a few sentences, three or less, of what you will have accomplished five years from now. Think big.

With that done, now I want you to write a numbered list of your one-year plan to get there. What are those major things you'll have to do this year to make that five-year vision a reality?

Five Years from Now

_____

_____

_____

_____

One Year Plan to Get There?

_____

_____

_____

Career and Business

1. _____

2. _____

3. _____

Hobbies and Side Hustles

  1. _____

  2. _____

  3. _____

Friends and Family

  1. _____

  2. _____

  3. _____

Health and Fitness

  1. _____

  2. _____

  3. _____

Attitude and Character

  1. _____

  2. _____

  3. _____

Wealth and Finance

  _____

1. _____

2. _____

3. _____

Spiritual and Self

1. _____

2. _____

3. _____

Skills You Need

Create a bulleted list of the skills you'll need to realize your one-year and five-year vision. You already have skills listed from the last chapter. Put them here, in your one-year plan. If anything new comes to mind, list them in this bulleted list with the ones you've already come up with. Here's what mine looks like:

Writing — Read one book on writing a month. Read one fiction book a month. Take note of what I'm picking up and use it in my own writing that day.

Character — Study those qualities in others that I want in myself, whether from movies or real life. Try those qualities on for size myself for a few days. See if it sticks.

Skills You'll Need

1. _____

2. _____

3. _____

4. _____

5. _____

6. _____

Action Plan

To give yourself a bit of momentum in the upcoming year, make an action plan for your next 30 days. What are those things you could do before the end of the first month of the year that would bring you a quick win, build your momentum for the next 11 months, and set you on a path for success by the end of next year?

Action Plan

1. _____

2. _____

3. _____

4. _____

5. _____

This is your yearly plan. If this is your first time doing something like this, it may take an hour or more to do. But that hour spent now will pay off dividends in the year to come. You'll review this plan monthly so it's always top of mind, front and center, and to ensure you are always on task.

This document, wherever you keep it, should be available at all times. Especially for those monthly reviews, and for times of need. There will be points along the way in your year where you'll doubt your plan, where you'll encounter failures. It's at those times this document will reinvigorate you, focus you, and make it clear what you are trying to accomplish and how it will feel when you get there.

Plan Your Month

With your plan for the year in place, you can now construct a monthly plan for how to get there. We're not going to worry about all 12 months right now. Too many things will change from month to month to waste time re-planning. We're just going to focus on the upcoming month, taking it one month at a time.

While it may be tempting to wait until the beginning of the month to plan things out, I find that this already puts me a step behind. So, instead, we'll plan for the upcoming month on the last day of the current month. By looking at the month ahead, you enter into the new month with an established plan. You can hit the ground running.

If you've broken down your goals into 12 milestones, as discussed earlier in this chapter, your job will be simple:

1. Set your goals for the upcoming month

2. Set what habits you will develop this month

3. Set what skills will you focus on learning this month

Set Your Goals for the Upcoming Month

Write down the milestone you wish to achieve this month. One that aligns with your broken-down goals for the year. What goals do you need to have achieved by the end of the month to be on track for achieving your goals by the end of the year?

For my $1.5 million sales target, I knew I needed to have sold $125,000 worth of product to be on track. That was my goal for the month, and throughout the month, I could track to that goal. Every time I looked at my monthly plan, I'd see that number ($125,000) staring me in the face daily. But this wasn't my only goal.

I had goals for health and fitness, friends and family, and every other important aspect of my life. Having gone through Chapter Seven, you should have these goals too. Write down your monthly goals for each area of your life such that, by achieving them, you will be on track for the year.

Monthly Goals

Health and Fitness: _____

Friends and Family: _____

Wealth and Finances: _____

Spiritual and Self: _____

Hobbies and Side Hustles: _____

Attitude and Character: _____

Career and Business: _____

Set the Habits You Will Develop This Month

Based on the habits you wish to learn this year, write down the specific habits you will work on this month. If you use a habit tracker like the one shown below, fill in your habits here. Simple pen and paper works great and is what I use. Every day gets a row, every habit gets a column, and the intersections get filled in every day I finish tracking to that habit.

In case you are wondering why we're only capturing habits for the current month, it's because we can't predict exactly where we'll be in the future. Bad habits may develop. Good habits may not be as useful as others. If we simply kept the same habits all year and never reviewed them, we might find ourselves with a bundle of bad habits that have accumulated and a few good habits that just aren't doing their job anymore.

In the last part of this book, we will discuss how to review your habits, double-down on good ones, and eliminate bad ones. This review will happen on a monthly basis. For now, just write down the habits that you'll need to work on in the upcoming month, like in the example below.

	Read Book	Practice Writing	Exercise	Eat Healthy	Wake up early	Plan my day	Meditate	Journal	Practice Gratitude
January 01	X	X	X	X		X	X	X	X
January 02	X	X		X		X	X	X	X
January 03	X	X	X		X	X		X	X
January 04		X	X	X	X	X	X	X	X
January 05	X	X	X		X	X	X	X	X

Grab the downloadable Home Early Habit Tracker on www.michaelmehlberg.com/homeearly.

Set the Skills You Will Learn This Month

If you need to learn a new skill to make achieving your goals easier, set a goal to learn that skill for the upcoming month. Depending on what you need to learn, perhaps reading a book or weekly calls with a mentor will do the trick. Think about all the ways you could acquire a new skill quickly, and track it as a lead measure by adding a new daily goal to the list of habits you've already created above.

Just like your goal breakdown, you can breakdown the skills that are too big to learn in a single month by setting month-sized milestones for them. Take writing for example. Writing this book is squarely within my purpose, vision, and goals. As such, becoming a better writer is a skill I want to learn. So, for my monthly plan, I have "Learn How to Write Better" as a skill. To do that, I'm going to read a book on writing every day. The book I've selected to read is 137 pages long. There are 31 days this month, which means I'm adding a goal to read 4.4 pages per day to my habit tracker. Every day I read 4.4 pages or more, I check the box as having finished that daily goal. By the end of the month, I'll have read a book and increased my knowledge on writing.

Plan Your Week

Just as you planned your month to ensure you were on track to achieve your goals by the end of the year, you'll now plan your week to make sure you are on track by the end of the month. And, just like we planned at the end of the month instead of the beginning, we'll do our weekly planning every Sunday night, looking at the workweek ahead. If you'd rather reserve Sunday for family and resting, do your planning at the end of your work week. Friday before leaving home from work is a good time. Whatever you do, don't wait until Monday morning. Monday morning is too late, and you're likely to get pulled in 47 different directions before you have a chance to plan a single minute. If that happens, the whole week will go by without a plan becoming a disorganized and chaotic mess like before.

This part of the planning should be considerably easier, though slightly more tactical. Namely because your habit tracker for the month is already developed, your skills are already set, and your monthly goals are established. But also because we're moving from strategic planning to more immediate scheduling. So, let's figure out where you need to be by the end of the week to ensure you are on track to achieving your monthly goals:

1. Set your objectives for the week

2. Create daily actions and milestones

3. Schedule your days

Set Your Objectives for The Week

Just like when you planned for where you want to be by the end of the month, let's set objectives for where you need to be by the end of the week. This may entail breaking down your month into four (one for each week) milestones that, once accomplished, add up to a finished monthly goal. If, for example, you have an objective to get a website up and running from ground zero by the end of the month, you may need to buy the domain in week one, install the web software on week two, collect the home page graphics and copy by the end of week three, and put it all together in week four.

You don't need a detailed plan for the week after next, or the week after that. Just focus on the upcoming week at hand, making sure it ties into your goals for the month.

Create Daily Actions and Milestones

With your weekly objectives in place, you can figure out where you need to be at the end of each day such that you accomplish those objectives by the end of the week. For each area in your life, you need to know where you should be at the end of each day. Write it on your calendar. These daily objectives are going to be the most important thing for any given day. They are the work that matters.

Schedule Your Days

In the next chapter, we'll get into planning vs. scheduling. For now, just look at your upcoming week and block off time to get these daily objectives—your important work—done. You already have daily objectives that are based on completing a larger objective by the end of the week, an even larger objective finished by the end of the month, and your main objective complete by the end of the year. If you don't block off time to get those daily objectives done, you'll lack for time to work on them. Another busy week will take the place of a productive one.

Once you've blocked off your most important work, look ahead to your calendar. What events do you have to deal with? Are they all required? Can any of them be moved around and/or grouped together at more convenient times? If you're so inclined, think about what you want to get out of each meeting. Even if it's time with family or an outing with friends, think through what your purpose is for taking the time to meet up. Imagine the perfect outcome. Write it down (right in the calendar event if you wish) to solidify it in your mind and give you something to review before you head into that meeting, refreshing you on the purpose of spending your time before the event.

With your year, month, and week planned, you've done all you can do to prepare yourselves for actual work. Now we need to carve out time to actually do it. Which is exactly where scheduling comes in.

Chapter Eleven

Planning vs. Scheduling

"If it's not on your calendar, it's not a priority. If you don't have goals for it, you're probably not thinking about it. If you're not thinking about it, then it's probably falling apart."

—Benjamin Hardy

R emember Franklin Planners? My Dad used to tote one everywhere. Bound in leather and stuffed thick with assorted papers, it was the executive professionals' badge of the 1990s.

I remember spying it on the kitchen counter, wondering at its contents, imagining it packed full of world-changing business deals, c-level contacts at publicly traded companies, and strategic plans for supreme corporate domination. Alas, when I grew old enough to afford my own, Franklin Planners were no longer in vogue, replaced instead by their digital equivalent, the Palm Pilot. I bought this digital copycat, learned how to write its semi-cryptic letters, and didn't look back for 15 years. Now, I see there was always something missing.

The Palm Pilot was *not* the digital equivalent of a paper planner. Neither are its successors: the BlackBerrys, the Surface Books, or the iPhones of the world. Something was lost in the translation from paper to silicon. The most important part of a planner. The ability to plan.

There's a difference between planning and scheduling. Planning is what we just did. It's thinking about what you want your life to look like in one, three, five, ten, or twenty years. Where do you want to be? What do you want to have? What do you want to be doing? Scheduling, on the other hand, is what you do today, tomorrow, or this week. Plans are your mission, your vision, your goals. Schedules are your meetings and other calendar events. They are the blocked off times where you do the work necessary to achieve your goals.

For example, my *plan* for tomorrow might be to refurnish our dining room. My *schedule* will be to go to Costco at 9 am, spend an hour shopping for and buying a dining room table, driving home at 10 am, unloading and putting the thing together at 10:30 am, then spending the next two hours painting the dining room, have a 12:30 pm lunch for 30 minutes, hang a new light fixture at 1 pm for one hour, then playing video games until bed.

If you have a plan without a schedule, you'll have good intentions without action. This leaves you vulnerable to getting lost in a sea of urgent tasks that distract you from your goals. You'll want to buy a dining room table but may wake up late and get to Costco when it's a fucking zoo, taking two hours instead of one. You'll have to interrupt your painting with lunch and then might lose yourself to the mental pit of Instagram for a bit. Before you know it, it'll be 5 pm and you'll have wet walls, a half-hung light fixture, and nowhere to eat.

On the other hand, if you have a schedule without a plan, you'll work hard toward an unknown goal and make progress toward someone else's vision. You'll drive to Costco to just shop... for anything. You might buy a book; you might buy one of their thick and meaty hot dogs. You won't get your dining room started. You'll leave and spend the next hour with stomach pain in the bathroom reading your new book.

Build your plan first (which you should have already done), then schedule daily (which we'll do now). Create a direction for yourself, then block time to execute. Design your life, then live it.

#

The beauty of scheduling what needs to get done is this: Your time is blocked, making it far less likely that distractions, meetings, or other people will take it. When you schedule a task, you're more inclined to work on it. When you schedule a task, others can't capitalize on your time without your permission.

Imagine two scenarios. In scenario one, you have a free and open calendar. You've got goals, and you've even broken those goals down. You know what you *should* be working on today but are giving yourself all day to do it. What happens when the phone rings, when someone comes to the door, or when a new email comes in?

When the phone rings, it's easy to think, I wonder what the caller needs? I can probably help them. I'll just answer it. When someone comes to your door, you have no reason to turn them away. After all, your calendar is clear; you'll just get to your important work later. When an email comes in, it's far too enticing to triage it immediately. You get bonus points for being responsive, and now your inbox has one less to-do to deal with.

The problem with this approach is that you're not doing your important work. You're not even doing *your* work. You're doing other peoples' work. You're replacing your goals with whatever urgent matter someone else has brought to your attention.

In scenario two, you get a knock at the door, a phone call, an email, but you have something on your calendar. You only have so much time to finish before your next meeting. If you don't work on it now, there'll be no time to squeeze it in since the rest of your day is scheduled.

These interruptions are far easier to control. You can simply ignore that call and set a reminder to call them back later. You can tell the person at your door that you really need to get something done, but you'll stop by later to see what's up (or ask them to send you an email so you can work on their request later). You can set a time later to answer all your emails at once, removing the start/stop overhead of going to your email app, checking to see what's new, then trying to context-switch back to whatever it was you were doing (and risking getting sucked into the rabbit hole of email while you're in there).

Sure, some things will have to get addressed instantly. Your boss may come to your door with a time-sensitive matter. Your spouse may call and say the pipes exploded in your house and the basement is flooding with toilet water. An email may come in with a late bill notice, saying they're going to shut down your electricity if you don't pay immediately. Those are worthy distractions. But they'll be few and far between. The multitude of interruptions you face on a daily, even hourly basis are usually *never* emergencies. They can almost *always* wait. They can wait until you schedule them.

When you get to the end of the year, will you remember if you answered that email immediately? Will you remember that phone call? Will you remember what task you did for someone who came to your door unannounced? Likely not. But you *will* remember that you hit your goal. You *will* realize that you achieved all that you set out to achieve. You *will* have a new sense of direction and hope for the future—a future where you are in control of your schedule, your calendar, your goals, your focus, your vision.

Schedule Your Day

Years ago, while visiting San Francisco on a business trip, I arrived at my hotel just before midnight. I had an early morning so needed to get to bed but was too spun up from the natural hustle and bustle of travel to sleep. Not wanting to get involved with a Netflix show, I dug through a care basket left by the hotel staff and found what I now call a daily planning card.

This card was quite simple. It was the size of an index card with times printed along the left from 7 am to 9 pm in 30-minute increments. I filled it out, went to bed, and awoke to the most productive day I'd ever had. Ever.

Benjamin Franklin is well known for his daily plan, which he laid out in advance. Every morning, he'd rise at 5 am to the same daily ritual: work, read, work some more, rest, examine his day, and sleep. He is also well known for saying, "by failing to plan, you are planning to fail." Good advice from a legend. But he's not the only one. Alexander Graham Bell once said, "Before anything else, preparation is the key to success." Clearly these two gents held planning and preparation in high esteem.

Now, before you say that those two historical figures are out of touch with modern life, take note. Former American Express CEO,

Kenneth Chenault, lists three important things to finish the following day so he can wake up and immediately start working on what matters. In fact, in a survey of 163 corporate leaders from Fortune 500 companies, the average leader spent 25 minutes on strategy and planning every day (Rampton, 2014). If this anecdotal evidence isn't enough, researchers Bruce Britton and Abraham Tesser (1991) studied the effect of time management practices on college students' GPAs. Shockingly, they showed that time management skills were a bigger influence on GPA than high-school SAT scores.

The takeaway? Planning your day in advance is the single most effective thing you can do to produce consistency measurable results. And the process is dead simple.

If you're the detailed type who likes the idea of scheduling your day down to the last detail, keep reading. If you'd rather float through your day than plan it, skip Method #2. Need a little structure but don't like the idea of breaking down your day into 15-minute increments, skip to Method #3. Or, if you're like me and find that some days need detailed plans and others need general guidance, read them all so you can use the method that best fits your mood on any given day.

METHOD 1 // For the Detail-Oriented Nut Job (like me most days)

From the moment you wake up until the moment you retreat to bed, block your entire day in 15-minute increments with meetings, administrivia, thinking time, side projects, family obligations, hobbies, and rest. And yes, that means every fucking minute of your day is scheduled.

You'll block 15 minutes for making and taking that first sip of coffee. You'll block two 15-minute increments for showering and shaving and throwing on some deodorant. You'll block another two for lunch, another for prep for that one-hour meeting at 1 pm, and four 15-minute blocks for the meeting itself.

This method is not for the faint of heart. But if you take the time to plan in advance how every minute of your day will go, you can realize some massive benefits.

First, you'll never again complain of not having any downtime because you'll literally schedule it into your day. If you know that 15 minutes of surfing cat videos will put you in the right mood before that boring-ass corporate meeting, well then by God, watch a few of those fur babies do super cute things. Second, by planning your day in such incredible detail, you will be able to realize the benefits of thinking ahead. For example, if you have a 30 minute commute, you can "double-book" yourself by blocking off two 15-minute increments for the drive and those same two increments for listening to an audiobook (bonus points if you choose one that builds a skill).

Though a completely booked calendar sounds scary at first, once you realize you're in control of every moment, you'll find it's a productive and balanced way to work. You won't fall victim to distractions. You won't wish you could spend more time with your family, you'll actually block time to do so. Instead of working relentlessly without time to think, rest, and recharge, you will plan for adequate time to work *and* take breaks.

Step 1

Open your primary calendar app (pen and paper for us vintage and fancy types) and schedule your most important activities in free time slots. That could be family, your main job, or an exciting side project. You are literally booking an appointment with yourself for the tasks that matter most.

Note that this does *not* mean you should schedule your meetings first. I get it; people jam meetings on your calendar like I jam sausage stuffing in my mouth on Thanksgiving. But meetings are not your most important work. Your most important work gets highest priority. Always.

Also, make sure no single task is scheduled for longer than two hours. Stopping for a short rest is necessary to staying productive; you'll avoid boring your brain with one task, forcing its attention to wander, and losing valuable focus. Even if you have a grueling 8-hour task ahead, break it up into four blocks of two hours with 15-minute breaks in between.

Step 2

With your most important work scheduled, fill in the rest of your day with exercise, breakfast, lunch, dinner, breaks, etc. Do *not* over-schedule yourself. If it normally takes you 30 minutes to exercise, be sure to leave time on either side for putting on workout cloths, rinsing off the stink, and making your organic, glucose-free, herbal vegetable protein shake. If you normally spend 30 minutes for lunch, factor in time drive to and from Hardees for your food-coma burger, and time in the afternoon to nap it off.

Step 3

With any remaining time slots on your calendar, schedule hobbies and extracurricular activities, filling out your day completely. If you still have an extra time block or two, attend to your to-do list, plucking off the most important activities and scheduling them as you did your important work, hobbies, and other activities.

Don't Forget

It takes time to brush your teeth. It takes time to settle down for bed. It takes time to plan your day tomorrow. Add those things into your calendar up front. You know you are going to do them, so don't fool yourself into thinking you will watch Netflix until 10 pm then magically be in bed and sleeping by 10:01.

Keep in Mind

Without a doubt, the plan you make for the day will get off track. A meeting will run over. A task will take longer than expected. You'll spend 20 minutes watching YouTube videos instead of 15 because you can't stand the thought of listening to your boss drone on for an hour at the upcoming status meeting. That's fine. That's okay. Simply adjust your future blocks of time or move things around to accommodate. The point of planning your day isn't to follow the plan exactly. It's to think about what you need to do and block off the time to actually do it.

"Everyone has a plan until they get punched in the mouth."

— Mike Tyson

This is the method I use the most, But it's not the only way. If, like me, you enjoy having your day laid out in front of you, completely planned from the moment you wake until the time you go to bed, try it on for size. If this sounds insane, try something like this...

METHOD 2 // A Little Loosey, a Little Goosey

If you made it here, I've maybe convinced you that planning is important, but you're not about to lock in 64 15-minute meetings with yourself over 16 hours tomorrow. You want to get more important work done, but the thought of scheduling your every minute twists your panties in a bunch. You need more flexibility. You can't follow a strict schedule. No prob. This might be the method for you.

Step 1

Grab a small sheet of paper. An index card is perfect. Ask yourself, if you could get three things done tomorrow (and only three things) what would they be?

Step 2

You can't work on all three at once, so take a look at your list and circle the one you'll work on first.

Step 3

Flip the card over and list any other small tasks (phone calls to make, errands to run, etc.) that you'd like to work on if you have time.

With your three highest priority items front and center and your highest priority item circled, you can hit the ground running tomorrow. Starting with the highest, try to get all three high-priority tasks done by noon. At the very least, get the circled task done by then. Even if that's the only thing you get done, you'll have tackled your most important work first and feel great about your day. If you get all three done, you'll be singing like Bing Crosby on Christmas day.

Should you find yourself between major tasks and in need of a break, flip the card over and work on one of your smaller tasks in-between. Anything not done at the end of the day can carry over to your plan for tomorrow.

METHOD 3 // Structured, but Wiggly. Like Jell-O

Maybe a day full of 15-minute meetings sounds too stressful but floating through your day is too loosey-goosey for your style. Here's an in-between method for blocking your time and creating just enough to structure to thrive.

Step 1

Like the Loosey-Goosey method, choose the top three things you'd like to get done tomorrow; three tasks or projects that you can realistically complete that would make for an awesome day. Prioritize them.

Step 2

Make a list of errands, calls, and other administrative tasks you'd like to get done during the day. Prioritize these too.

Step 3

Open your favorite calendaring app (pen and paper counts) and block off the two to three most productive hours of your day. This will be a two- or three-hour meeting with yourself for that highest priority task.

Step 4

Rinse and repeat for your next highest priority task. In other words, for the second highest priority task on your list, schedule another big block of time for yourself to work on it. Be sure to leave time in between your time blocks for dicking around.

Now, instead of worrying about the clock, you can focus on your highest priority task or project and work on it until you need a break. It's important to focus only on that one task and not get distracted.

In fact, if you're getting distracted by notifications or other tasks in your list, you've probably scheduled too much time for your highest priority task. Just as your brain filters out a bad smell after a few minutes, so too does your brain filter out the thoughts you spend too much time attending to. Your brain grows accustomed to whatever activity you are engaged in and tunes it out in search of something more interesting, an interesting phenomenon known as the vigilance decrement.

The Vigilance Decrement

If you think that hunkering down to work harder, concentrate more, or labor longer is going to help you push through, you're wrong. Researchers at the University of Illinois at Urbana-Champaign found that our brains aren't built to focus for hours on end on one task; they're built to notice and respond to change. Your brain is always paying attention to something. It just has trouble paying attention to one thing for too long.

Think about walking into a room with a distinct odor, like an indoor pool or a sweaty locker room. At first much of your focus us on the smell. But over time, it fades into the background until you don't notice it at all. If asked, you could bring your attention back to the stink of chlorine and jock straps, but the longer you stay in that room, the more other sights, sounds, and smells draw your attention away.

This "vigilance decrement" is a drag to productivity. After all, if we could focus on a single task for 12 hours without distraction every day, we'd be best-selling authors, international chess masters, world renowned pianists, and 7-figure entrepreneurs. Since we can't, we must devise systems to manage our attention by feeding our brains a bit of what they crave: rest and something new to think about.

This is why popular time management methods like Pomodoro (which are really focus management techniques) are helpful. The Pomodoro method recommends 25-minute work periods followed by a 5-minute break. Other such methods, which are based on the same principles but that vary the time between work and rest, exist. Desktime recommends their 52/17 method, which is (surprise!) 52 minutes of work followed by a 17-minute break. Pulse and Pause recommends 90 minutes of work followed by a physiological rest period to recharge your depleted attention.

Which method you choose depends on how long you can concentrate without a break. My son, for example, can willfully ignore everything when reading a book or playing a video game. And I do mean everything. I once burned the shit out of some bacon while he read a new book. The room filled with charred black smoke, the fire alarm went off, and the dog started barking. He didn't even look up. While everyone else ran around opening doors and fanning the smoke alarm with dish towels, my oldest son sat unfazed, reading amidst a bacon haze while I stood in awe at his power of concentration.

I don't know anyone else who can concentrate like that, and I suspect this superpower of his is rare. Luckily, it's possible to increase our powers of concentration with mental exercise. Much like physical exercise can increase endurance and muscle mass, mental exercises can a) increase our ability to focus, and b) increase the length of time we can focus on one task before our brains start attending to other matters.

To do that, use one of the methods described above. The Pomodoro method is a good place to start. If 25 minutes of work feels like too much at first, reduce it to 20, 15, or even 10. Focus on one task for that period of time, then follow it with a five-minute break. When your break is over, go back to that original task for another 10, 15, 20, or 25 minutes of effort. Rinse and repeat this cycle four times, then take a longer, 15-minute break before starting it all over again. This method will not only help you stay focused on a single task (ideally an important task from your list of goals), but over time can increase your powers of concentration as you move from 10-minute work increments to 15, 20, 25, and beyond. Once you can concentrate without distraction for the full work increment, increase that it by five minutes. Like exercise, your minds focus muscle will grow to give you more focused work time during the day.

Tracking Habit Development

Remember those habits you wrote down in Chapter Nine? It's time to track them. Habits aren't performed every once in a while. They are performed daily, if not more. As such, tracking them daily helps you remember to do them and holds you accountable to yourself.

Tracking doesn't have to be complicated. It just has to happen. It can be as simple as a checkmark in a notebook or habit tracking app. The medium doesn't matter. What matters is that your habit tracker:

1. Is always available

2. Captures whether each habit is complete for the day

3. Keeps a visual history of how many days in a row your habits have been completed

Remember, it takes 66 days to transform a conscious task into a routine that can run on autopilot. Missing even a single day may extend that period of time. Missing a week may force you to start over. By visualizing how many days in a row you've completed our habits, you are holding yourself accountable. Breaking a day, and therefore putting a hole in your visual habit chart, will be off-putting.

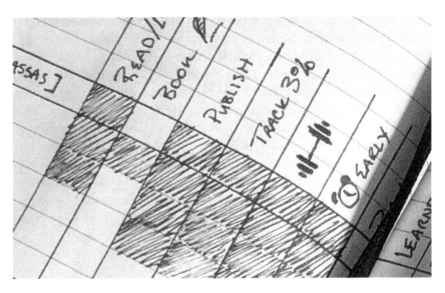

A simple pen and paper visualization tool is what I use. Each day has its own row, each important habit has its own column. Complete a habit, color in the box. Miss a habit, leave the box blank. It's a simple

yet effective tool for telling at a glance whether I'm actually building the habits that I believe are important to achieving my goals.

Tracking Skills Development

You created a list of skills in Chapter Nine. Now it's time to prioritize them, break them down, and track their development (and therefore *your* development) throughout the year.

Any skills that are mandatory to getting your most important work done should be the highest priority. After those, any skill that will significantly make achieving your goals easier comes next. Finally, the lowest priority skills (but still important) are those skills that will remove obstacles and reduce headaches.

Now, with your prioritized list, break down the development of these skills like you did with your goals in Chapter Seven. If you have a list of books to read, divide up the pages and set milestones throughout the year for reading them. If you have a skill that will forever be in development (like learning chess, guitar, or a new language), consider adding it to your habit tracker so you can track and make incremental daily progress.

Marketing and writing are two skills I identified long ago as being critical to my personal and professional development. For writing, I set a goal to read one writing book a month. For marketing, it's the same. At the end of each month, I choose the next book I'm going to read, figure out how many pages I need to read per day, and add that as a checkbox to my habit tracker to ensure I'm keeping pace.

As we already discussed, developing your skills is an important aspect to developing yourself and achieving goals that you never thought possible. But, just as Antoine de Saint-Exupéry said that "A goal without a plan is just a wish," a skill without a plan to develop it is the same.

Prioritize the skills you need to learn, break them down into meaningful milestones, and track them in your habit tracker to ensure you are making progress towards them every day.

PART IV

Protecting Your Time

Dealing with the onslaught of unavoidable distractions

"So it is: we are not given a short life but we make it short, and we are not ill-supplied but wasteful of it..." — Seneca

Chapter Twelve

Incoming!

"If we let ourselves, we shall always be waiting for some distraction or other to end before we can really get down to our work."

— C. S. Lewis

With three kids in baseball, I play a lot of catch. Every once in a while, my wife will join us, and we'll form a circle to pass the ball between us. Naturally, a conversation will start about school, work, or any number of activities planned for the upcoming weekend. And, just as naturally, one of us breaks attention from the game just long enough to miss it hurtling toward our face. Usually, it's me.

You know the feeling. Someone tosses an object your way thinking you're paying attention, but you're not. You're lost in thought until your brain rips you back to reality against your will, saving yourself from a bloody lip or a black eye. You don't think, you can't help it, you just react.

Our work and life often have the same effect. While busy focusing on something important, a notification comes ripping in against our will and without consideration for what we were doing. The screen lights up. The device dings. It's all we can do to maintain our focus on the task at hand. Most of the time, we can't help but glance at the notification to make sure it's not a proverbial baseball heading toward our face; an email from the boss, or an upset customer could ruin our day. A social media post we're tagged in could blow up or a breaking news article could leave us out of touch with what's happening if left unread. So, we feel obligated to check, just to see, just to stay on top of the latest and greatest, just to prevent any mishaps.

Unfortunately, unless we shun our digital devices and move back to the stone ages (not a productive option), we're stuck with these incoming attention bombs. It's best to learn how to deal with them effectively so they don't continue to do what they're doing to us today—wasting our time and killing our focus.

What Notifications do to our Focus

In one government study, NASA put 17 engineers in the same room and tasked them with building a spacecraft, no outside interruptions allowed. While a spacecraft normally took six months to design, this undistracted team completed theirs in nine hours. They caught mistakes immediately instead of waiting for feedback to circle back around in email. They didn't have to wait for multiple reviews every time a small change was requested. Everyone was there, within eye- and earshot, able to comment and make an immediate impact. In short, proximity between multiple people working on a complex task without interruption *significantly* reduces the amount of time it takes to complete that task.

Including emails, phone calls, text messages, social media, and people stopping by your desk all contribute to 56% of the distractions in our environment. The other 44% come from your own procrastination and wandering mind. In fact, the average amount of time anyone spends working on a single task without interruption is just over three minutes. Three minutes and five seconds to be exact (Reed, 2016; "Feeling distracted," 2019).

Once interrupted, we don't just get back to work. It takes us a full 23 minutes to regain focus ("Feeling distracted," 2019). That doesn't mean three minutes of working followed by 23 minutes of watching

Bob Ross paint another mountain landscape. It means three minutes working on one thing, getting distracted and beginning work on something unrelated, then three minutes later getting distracted again and picking up yet another task. Twenty-three minutes later, we have no idea what we were working on to begin with, have worked on seven disparate tasks, and have finished precisely none of them.

The changing context in which we work on any one task doesn't help. For example, to triage a text message, you must switch to your texting app. Whatever you were doing before—writing in your notebook, emailing on your computer, or talking with a colleague—is now lost. You've switched context to your text app. In three minutes, you'll switch again. How many times have you followed a new notification to social media, only to follow another notification over to text messages, then another to email, and then completely forgot what you were working on in the first place?

The same thing happens in the real world too. Someone comes into your office and hands you a document. You move some things around, sign it, give it back. Now your pen is in a different spot and your papers are shuffled. Not a big deal, and this hardly amounts to much time, but it interrupts your flow and prevents you from getting right back to where you left off. You need to reset your context, assuming you can before the next interruption comes in.

These little pockets of time spent procrastinating and constant context switching add up to one fourth of our entire workday. Two hours, gone, never to be replaced. Time that could have been use for productive effort.

We can't let this happen anymore. Whether email, meetings, social media, we need strategies to deal with these and other distractions and stay focused on our important work.

Dealing with Email

Most knowledge workers spend 28% of their week (13 hours) on email. That's more than two and a half hours every single day reading, sorting, deleting and otherwise managing messages; a tremendous amount of time and mental energy. Two and a half hours! Movies aren't that long anymore.

Of course, we need e-mail to communicate with others. But it can be a huge distraction. Email is, after all, a means to an end. It's a tool for getting work done but is not the work itself. It's also a tool that's just as likely to create work as it is to help finish it. Emails distract, and they do so on everyone else's schedule. Most of the time when you're working on something else and need to focus.

Don't get me wrong, e-mails need to be dealt with. But with so much time spent on a task that doesn't directly help us accomplish our goals, we need methods to minimize the amount of time we spend on it so we can focus on work that matters.

To start, try email batching. Instead of dealing with each email as it comes in, handle them at pre-scheduled times of the day. Instead of dropping everything and losing context on the task at hand, you can stay focused on your most important matters and deal with emails when (and only when) it's time. Set it for once a day, three times a day, or even five times a day. It doesn't matter. Just group all that otherwise random and intermittent emailing together into one or more time blocks so you can read, respond, sort, and delete in one fell swoop. The beauty of this method is, if you won't be responding to emails other than when you've scheduled, you can turn off email notifications or shut off automatic fetch altogether. Why be distracted and feel the pull of responding? Save battery life and avoid the temptation.

When you do sit down to deal with your emails, you'll be faced with the same decision for everyone: Do I deal with this now or later? In David Allen's *Getting Things Done*, he suggests dealing with an email immediately and without question if it'll take less than two minutes. This prevents you from wasting time deciding over and over again. You know, when you read the email, decide you don't have time for it, mark the email unread, then re-read it in the future having forgotten about its contents. This entire cycle is a waste of time. Not to mention, the likelihood you'll run through this cycle more than once is high, which will turn from minutes into hours that could have been used more effectively elsewhere.

You can drive otherwise lengthy emails into this two-minute bucket with canned responses. Frequently asked customer questions are a good example. Instead of writing a custom response to everybody, create a copy/paste folder in your notebook system. I use Notion.

When you find yourself answering similar questions, save that canned response in your copy/paste folder. Whenever an email comes in, grab your canned response and save a truckload of time and energy. Bonus points if you find a plug-in. TextExpander does a good job with this, but I've seen others use "Canned responses" in Gmail to do the same thing.

When it's not appropriate to use a canned response, consider whether you need to engage the person via email, or if a more efficient medium would work. Instead of getting into a long, drawn-out, back-and-forth written discussion, just call the person. Why bother taking all that time to write and edit your response only to have to read theirs when it comes back in? Just call them, kill the email thread, and solving the problem right then and there.

Speaking of not creating more emails for yourself, why not try unsubscribing from all those newsletters that once seemed like a good idea but now just fill your inbox with tired ideas. When you get an email from a company you no longer read, unsubscribe immediately. It should take less than two-minutes (fitting into David Allen's two-minute rule above), and the few seconds you spend doing so will multiply. Every moment you don't have to decide, read, and delete yet another newsletter is a moment saved for real work. Don't want to unsubscribe because you fear you'll you'd be missing out? Nonsense. You can always re-subscribe later when you have the time and energy to deal with it.

Of the emails you do decide to keep, use the sort bar to process them by subject instead of by delivery time. Dealing with emails on the same subject will save you valuable thinking cycles and may even reduce the number you need to respond to. Many times, multiple people on the same thread add their inputs to a single topic. You can reply to one, answer everyone's questions at once, and get the hell outta there.

Finally, it's time to stop organizing your emails. Keeping one giant inbox and learning to use the advanced search functionality of your email client will pay dividends. Gmail, Outlook, and every other decent email system in existence has search parameters that can narrow down emails with attachments, between certain dates, with specific subjects, and having certain keywords in the body. Learning those search terms alone will allow you to find 99.9% of your emails in seconds. Do that, and you don't have to spend a single second moving emails around into different folders or tagging them with colorful categories.

Meetings, a Second Offender

"If you had to identify, in one word, the reason why the human race has not achieved and never will achieve its full potential that word would be 'meetings'."

— Dave Barry

My apologies in advance for getting a bit worked up here. It's just that meetings are a *huge* time sync. In fact, most managers spend up to ten hours a week in meetings, and some studies have shown the combined cost of meetings throughout the nation is around $37 billion every year (Montini, 2014). That's a lot of fucking time and a lot of fucking cash.

I'd like to say the answer is to simply eliminate meetings altogether. In fact, in Chapter Fourteen, I will literally help you say "no" to meetings (and a few other time-wasting activities). For now, instead of saying "no," ask yourself (and the meeting organizer) if a meeting is really necessary. Many times, a quick phone call or face-to-face chat with a colleague can resolve the matter at hand.

When it's not possible to replace a meeting with a chat, consider bundling your meetings together, back-to-back. There's nothing worse than having multiple meetings spaced just far enough apart that you can't get anything done. With 30 minutes between meetings, there's not much else you can do other than check email or get lost in asinine TikTok videos. You're losing productivity, not getting into a groove, and blowing time until your next meeting starts. Like batching emails, batching meetings back-to-back is far more productive to your overall schedule.

Oh, and for God sakes, if you're going to accept a meeting and spend the time attending it, make sure the meeting has a clear objective and agenda. Objectiveless, agendaless meetings are the biggest time suck of any office. Assuming you're the one setting up the meeting, putting an objective and agenda in the invite will help others understand what they should bring to make it productive. This saves everyone's time and energy, including yours, and gives you a reason to send anyone who isn't prepared back to their desk to get their shit together. Okay, that may be too harsh, but it's your time, not time. If you're attending someone else's meeting that doesn't have an objective or agenda, it's perfectly reasonable to send a polite email asking for either (or both). Tell the meeting organizer you'd like to understand what the meeting should accomplish and what topics will be covered so you can come prepared. Also, ask them what role they expect you to play in the meeting. Many times, you'll find either they don't know or someone else will fit the bill better, so you can respectfully bow out.

Finally, start on time, end on time, and stay focused throughout. You're there for a purpose, so stay focused on that purpose and end with purpose. If another topic worthy of discussion comes up, don't chase it down. Note it, take an action to schedule a follow-up meeting, and move on with the agenda at hand.

Above all else, remember, even if it's not your meeting, it is your time. It's literally your time! If the conversation is lagging, you are getting pulled off topic, or the agenda and objective of the meeting are falling apart, take the helm and steer things back on track. If the meeting organizer doesn't take the hint (they usually will), you'll be able to take charge, guide the meeting to land, and get back to your cat videos. Which is what we'll discuss next.

Social Media, The Worst Offender

I once went on a 365-day social media writing challenge to "find my writing voice." Every day, I'd pull up Instagram, snap a picture of something inspiring, and write a short article in the caption. I couldn't write much. Instagram allows only 2200 characters max. But between a full time job, a family with three kids, and writing this book, keeping my writing time to a minimum was necessary anyways.

Some days, when pressed for time, I'd knock out a two or three hundred word article in under 30 minutes. Other days, it seemed to take hours. I'd find myself frantically typing at midnight, hours after I wanted to go to bed, in hopes of accomplishing my goal of "just one article per day." After a week of this, I knew something was off.

The days I had extra time to spare were spent surfing Instagram instead of writing in it. Though I'd start up the app with every intention to write, I'd get caught up in my feed and scroll through image after image looking for something fun to watch, an inspiring picture to like, or a useful product to buy. I was procrastinating. I wasn't using Instagram; Instagram was using me.

Too often, that's how social media goes. One minute, you're recording videos, responding to comments, and doing your job. The next minute you're scrolling through your news feed looking for cat videos or some political commentary to spin you up.

That's because social media is addictive. The anticipation of a funny post, a heartwarming post, or an emotionally charged political post gives you a small dopamine hit. This makes you feel good about what you might encounter, so you start scrolling. Sure enough, one of your 500+ friends and followers posts something extremely interesting. Your anticipation comes true and your dopamine center gives you a nice little chemical-induced reward. It feels great, you anticipate more, you scroll and find more, rinse and repeat.

Unfortunately, trying to fight this addiction directly may not work. Not for long, at least. If you've ever set social media time limits on your phone, you know it's far too easy to blow past the limit and spend another 20 minutes cyberloafing by simply entering your password. No, your first defense can't be to lock yourself out. It's to prevent the addiction from ever taking hold in the first place.

Unless social media is part of your job, removing notifications to these apps won't hurt in the least. Anytime you open your social media app, you'll have all your updates, messages, and news feed right there, ready for your viewing pleasure. But by removing notifications, you'll be able to control when and where you start your social media frolic instead of getting pulled in by a single notification that leads to 20+ minutes of surfing every other notification you missed. Like meetings and emails, social media is best batched instead of consumed ad hoc.

Which means you must schedule time for it. Specifically, around your breaks. If you have time scheduled to kick back and relax with your favorite social media app, you won't feel as much pressure to log in and procrastinate important work at other times. You'll still get to check in and participate in the social sphere but will do it at pre-scheduled times. Times when you know you'll need a break.

When used like this, social media becomes a productivity enhancer. It gives you that short recharge you need to get back to productive work. Just be sure you have a start *and* end time for your social media adventures. It's easy to keep on scrolling through your feed, afraid that you'll miss out on something important (you won't). When your timer goes off and your productive time starts back up, honor it.

Finally, if you're serious about setting and keeping social media limits, have a friend or spouse set you app limit password in secret. And, if you're craving social interaction, call a friend or relative. If you have a fear of missing out, realize that whatever you found over the past 20 minutes of surfing, partially driven by that fear of missing out, didn't result in any amazing revelations and 100% won't in the next 20 minutes either.

If you're in the business of using social media for work, don't fall into the same trap that caught me. However, if you're just a casual user, take even more care. After all, the entire reason you use social media is to kick back, relax, get your mind off your job or the pressures of home life, and otherwise catch up on news. All those reasons are great reasons. There's no use in taking a hard stance against social media, shunning it from our lives completely. But we should take care to manage it appropriately so we don't look up from surfing and find that 45 minutes of our life is now gone, and we'll be staying late at work again to catch up on lost time.

Spend some time acknowledging this addictive behavior, understanding why you're feeling the way you're feeling, and figuring out a way to replace that feeling with the same feeling from somewhere more productive.

Budgeting Time for the Unknown

In the world of software engineering, traditional teams used to be treated like construction companies. Pour the foundation, put up the frame, brick the outside, add the roof, etc. But software engineering isn't like building a house. It's a creative endeavor, one that requires constant communication and managing unknowns, making it difficult to predict how long anything will take to finish.

If a project estimate is no better than a guess, we're setting ourselves up for feelings of guilt and unrealistic expectations of success. Worse, if we get behind schedule, we have to work late or rush to catch up (assuming either is possible).

To manage these unknowns and prevent a mad dash at the end of a project, Ken Schwaber and Jeff Sutherland developed a software engineering process called Scrum in the early 1990's. Their aim was to better manage unknowns and get more predictable, more consistent results.

One important aspect of Scrum is establishing a feedback loop to help us budget and account for lost time while setting appropriate expectations for how much we can accomplish. After all, if we continually set and miss our goals, it's not only hurtful to our success, it's impossible to maintain control over our work and is devastating to our mindset. With this feedback loop in mind, we're going to think through how much time we have available at the onset of a project and how much of that time might be taken up by unknowns.

Starting with the total amount of working time (in hours) you have available for the month (usually around 160), briefly think through everything that might interrupt that time. Things like meetings, vacations, sickness, random interruptions from colleagues, etc. Nothing is off limits. If it will take your time away from your work, list it, and estimate how much. Subtract that number from your total working time.

From there, list every task and how long each will take to complete. When this task list is complete, you will have filled up your remaining working time with all the necessary, prioritized, important tasks you need to get done in the following month. That's when you can get to work.

At the end of your working month, look back, assessing how many tasks you finished. If you *added* tasks because you had extra time, you probably overestimated the number and length of obstacles and distractions to your work. If you had *unfinished* tasks at the end of the month, you may not have accounted for enough.

Over the course of a few months, you'll get a sense for how much you can accomplish in a future month of work. If you're a nerd like me, you can track your estimation vs. actual time spent and get an average to use in future planning.

For example, early in my career, while running a small software engineering team using Scrum, we collected 12 months of estimates and actuals. We found that, on any given month, 55% of our time was consumed by... well, we had no idea what. Over half of our time was lost to unknown interruptions, meetings, vacations, sickness, web surfing, and social media chicanery. We tried fixing it but couldn't find any big offenders. So, we just accounted for it. With this 55% in mind, we could set realistic expectations for how much we could get done over the course of a month. We'd set challenging yet realistic goals, we'd feel accomplished at the end of each month, and we'd gain working momentum for the next month.

Use this time-budgeting method to better estimate how much work you can get done in a given day, week, month, and year. As you learn what an average amount of work and interruptions look like, you can factor that into future plans.

Stop beating yourself up for not achieving expectations that were unknowingly set too high in the first place. Time budget daily and you'll quickly get a feeling for what's realistic to accomplish tomorrow and the next day. Time budget weekly and you'll learn how many larger tasks or mini projects you can get done in a week (and how many you can't). Time budget over the course of a month and you'll start to notice unrealistic goals, get a feel for how many tasks you can actually get done in a month, and set yourself up for realistic expectations of future success.

> "Most people overestimate what they can do in a year and underestimate what they can do in two or three decades."
>
> — Tony Robbins

Chapter Thirteen

Managing What's Out of Your Control

"So the pie isn't perfect? Cut it into wedges. Stay in control, and never panic."

— Martha Stewart

When I started by first job, managing emails was a breeze. In the late '90s, email was far from the primary source of business communication. Zero-inbox was a thing. Every day. Because there were so few emails flying around, they were trivial to triage, and I was able to deal with the emails that arrived immediately.

As an added bonus, because so few emails were sent, it was easy to remember who owed me a response. Though any email fell out of my control the moment I clicked send, I could reasonably count on a response in a timely manner.

I dealt with the emails that came in. My colleagues dealt with theirs. Everyone was happy.

Today, email is a problem. We receive dozens, if not hundreds of emails daily, and send just as many. Most email apps are great at dealing with incoming requests. Emails are marked unread until you read them, at which point you can archive or move them to another folder. But outgoing emails, well, those just sit in your sent folder; a huge unorganized list of every email you've sent to anyone. Ever. And, while many emails we send are informative—existing only to let someone know where to meet, what number to call, or what's going on—other emails, especially those directly relate to our goals, require a response.

Unfortunately, like you and me, other people are busy. We can't rely on them to respond 100% of the time. Without a way to manage our sent mail folder, any tasks we delegate will be forgotten.

Instead of sitting back and accepting silence as a response, set a reminder. For every outgoing email that asks for a response, set a reminder for an appropriate time to follow up. Every email delegating a task gets a reminder too.

Once set, forget about it. You don't have worry about them or remember them. Eventually, your reminder will fire on schedule, jogging your memory of your original request and guiding you to the correct next step (call them, email them, go pound on their door and demand that they stop making you wait for their response, etc.).

Using this system, you can delegate a task or make a request without relinquishing responsibility for its completion. And, while you can't force others to provide that response, you can pester them until it becomes clear you're not going to forget.

And, as one final trick, you can extend this system beyond email. Make a request via phone, snail mail, or in person? Just set a reminder with your favorite app or email yourself the details and flag it to remind you at the right time.

Context Matters

Where you are, what tools you are using, what time of day it is, and who you're with are all considerations when seeking productivity. Take location, for example. If you're traveling to a city where a current customer works, it might be worth stopping by to keep the relationship fresh. This is location context. You don't triage emails when you're commuting, you do it when you're at your desk. You're not productive dialing into a teleconference from a rock concert, you take the call behind closed doors. Location contexts like these are handled naturally, but other contexts require a bit more forethought.

In the context of your car, you might plan to listen to podcasts and audiobooks while driving. In the context of sitting at your desk, there might be a dozen or more tasks you can perform to make progress toward your goals.

People have context too. One for your boss or colleagues, for example, allows you to plan on being productive with these individuals before meeting them. By keeping a list of things you need to discuss, you can kill two birds with one stone the next time you meet up.

Contexts are a low-cost way to maximize your burning candle, and they don't have to be contained to the workplace. What would you like to talk about with your kids when driving them to baseball practice? What can do for your spouse to deepen your relationship the next time you're together? When these ideas come to mind, whether for work, relationships, in your car, at your desk, or any other context, capture them in a note for that context. The next time, before entering into that context, review that note to deepen those relationships, make progress toward your goals, and get shit done.

Chapter Fourteen

Protecting Your Time

"Somewhere along the line, we allowed people to do whatever they wanted with our time. When this happens, their inefficiency becomes our inefficiency. Their wasted time becomes our wasted time."

— Craig Jarrow

The first time my son told me "no," I did what every parent does. I scolded him. Of course, that didn't end it. My son continued to say "no" every chance he could. And I continued to reinforce that "no" is *not* something you tell your own father.

All three of my children went through the same phase; saying "no" because they learned it, then saying "no" for a reaction, then saying "no" to be defiant. But, with time and a mountain of patience, we trained the little buggers and they now know that saying "no" is unacceptable. They can ask for more time on the PlayStation, they can state their case for spending the night at a friend's house, they can request a third scoop of ice cream, but outright saying "no" means big trouble.

From an early age, we've all been scolded for saying "no." We're expected to listen to our parents, follow our teachers' directions, and respect the authorities. And by and large, this works. When parents and teachers and police officers are looking out for our best interests, it's ill-advised to disregard them, let alone defy them.

But when we become adults, we don't often interact with our parents. We no longer go to school. And we (hopefully) don't often encounter the police. Yet the desire to acquiesce continues. Every path in our brain has been trained to say "yes." So, when a colleague calls asking for help reviewing his email, you say "yes." When someone throws a two-hour meeting on your calendar with no agenda, you blindly accept. When your boss has a new idea and wants you to implement it immediately, you say "sure."

We agree to take on these tasks because, even though we have our own things to do, it's hard to say "no." We like to help others. It makes us feel good. It makes us look good. On top of that, we agree because, well, maybe we do have the time. Our calendar isn't blocked up with meetings, so sure, let's meet. Your colleague sounded worried about his email, so you'd hate to turn him down. You think:

- I've got nothing better to do, or

- that other commitment I have (which isn't here to defend itself) can wait, or

- my family is always there for me and will understand if I get home a bit late tonight.

As such, we become our own worst enemies. We allow others to have a say in how our time is spent, what we do, and therefore how we live.

This is a mistake. Since you can't add more time to your day, you can't doom yourself to overcommitment without losing something in return. You've got to know when enough is enough. When you've got too much on your plate. Even if you *can* do it all, overcommitment is a recipe for low quality output and stressful working and living.

"We need to learn the slow 'yes' and the quick 'no.'"

— Warren Buffett

What's more, saying "yes" to everything becomes a self-fulfilling problem. You become an easy target for others to make more requests and ask you for more help. You will either a) become exhausted over time as you simultaneously work on your own tasks while trying to please everyone around you, or b) you will begin to resent others for your inability to say "no" as you work on the tasks that make them successful at the expense of your own. Neither of these is a healthy or productive way to live.

You have a right to decline. At the very least, you have a right to take on a new task, fulfill a new request, or accept a new challenge *after* considering how it will affect your plan for the future.

It's simple really. If you want more clarity, focus, and progress toward your goals, you need to protect your time.

"If you don't prioritize your life, someone else will."

— Greg McKeown, Essentialism: The Disciplined Pursuit of Less

Luckily, everything you've done thus far to create your vision, set your goals, and develop a daily plan have laid the groundwork for protecting your time. But that still doesn't make it any easier.

Saying "no" is a delicate task, especially when doing so to people whom you respect, whom respect you, or whom have authority over you. Saying "no" to the wrong person can be a fatal job or relationship mistake if not handled carefully.

Fortunately, there are plenty of ways to gracefully say "no" when a request for your time doesn't fit with the work that matters to you. And you must be graceful when you say "no." After all, people ask you for help because they respect you, love you, like you, or believe you can help them in some way. That's amazing responsibility. It takes vulnerability to ask for help. It takes trust. Be grateful for it. Accept it. Encourage it. But be conscious of how it will drive you as a person, your goals, your vision.

With that in mind, it's easy to realize that saying "yes" when you mean "no" isn't the honorable thing to do. If you're not truly committed, you'll resist the request to the end. You won't be able to fully commit yourself. You will deliver lackluster results. In turn, this will be worse than overcommitting yourself in the long run. You'll gain a reputation for poor work, inadequate results, or being disingenuous. Turning down someone else's request only hurts for a moment. Being known as someone without integrity follows you for a long, long time.

So, let's look at some reasons why saying "no" is so hard and break down solutions to them one-by-one, starting with the fear of missing out.

The Fear of Missing Out

We don't always say "no" to please others. Sometimes we say it out of fear—a fear of missing out. Fear of missing out, or FOMO, is a real phenomenon. FOMO drives us to click on article after article on the web in search of a secret tactic that will help us get where we're going. It's the reason we jump at a new opportunity without consideration, even if it takes us off the path to our destination.

One Black Friday, when sales were out-of-control-awesome and I was spending money like Rihanna in a gold tooth store, FOMO took me over hard. I was sitting on the couch when a notification popped up on my screen for a sale on an iPhone App called GuitarTabs: "Subscribe now, 50% off, deal only lasts until midnight!"

I have a guitar in my office but hadn't played since college 20 years prior. I had downloaded the free app in hopes of playing a few songs during Christmas break, but quickly found a dozen other things to do such as write this book, spend time with family, buy presents, etc.

Regardless, when that notification popped up, my fear of missing out took over. What if I wanted to learn a new song? What if the price went back up and I regretted it later? What if I bumped into John Mayer on a flight to LA and was offered a background guitar player gig? I'd need this app, right? And so, without thinking, I subscribed for a year. I haven't used it since.

FOMO takes many forms. Buying yearly subscriptions to apps you won't use. Clicking on web articles you don't need to read. Worrying about news headlines that can in no way affect your life. You might fear not being in "the know," so you tune into the news and find yourself scrolling through headlines 30 minutes later, unable to resist that next big story. You might be afraid of missing an opportunity to look good in front of someone you respect. You imagine what they're doing is important, meaningful, or will gain you notoriety. So, you say "yes" to their request without considering how your own goals will suffer.

But will reading that news article really help you achieve your vision? If you were to prioritize "looking good" among everything else, would it be at the top (or anywhere near it)? Will the notoriety you gain from helping someone with their request help you get to your goals faster? Likely no, no, and no.

Learn to recognize the fear of missing out. And, when you do, ask yourself if what you fear missing out on will help you reach your goals faster. In other words, if you added this request to your list and had to prioritize it, would it be at the top of the stack?

Just remember, if you are focused on what matters, then any request or article or app or opportunity is the equivalent of scope creep, no matter how much you fear missing out on it. If it doesn't fit into your goals, then you're not truly missing out on anything.

The Best Offense…

I'm going to assume you've seen the movie Office Space. If you haven't, stop reading and go watch it this instant.

One of the greatest scenes in this movie (or any movie) is when Peter scrambles to finish work before his boss, Bill Lumberg, stops by. Peter knows Lumberg will ask him to stay late. What's worse, he knows he won't be able to say "no." So he rushes to pack everything up and jet from his cubicle before getting caught. Except his computer struggles to shut down and he fumbles with his bag. Just as his ass leaves the seat, Lumberg stops Peter dead in his tracks, one step from a weekend of freedom.

"Hello Peter, whaaaat's happening? Ummmm, I'm gonna need you to go ahead and come in tomorrow, so if you could be here arounnnndddd nine, that'd be great, mkay?"

Peter failed to get out of the office in time. But he knew that, when it comes to protecting his time, the best offense is a good defense. In

Peters case, his defense was getting out the door before Lumberg showed up. In our case, we need to erect multiple safeguards to protect our time before the proverbial (or literal) boss man stops us from getting home early.

The first defense, as we saw in Chapter Eleven, is to block your time. Every moment of it. Every meeting, every task, every event needs to be on your calendar. During your daily planning and scheduling, fill your every waking minute with activities in time blocks the size of your choosing.

If your organization uses shared calendars or free/busy calendars like Outlook, blocking your time is sometimes the only way to prevent it from getting sucked up by others. If colleagues can't find a time on your calendar, they'll simply look for another one. Sure, they may email and ask if you can move things around, but if your time is blocked, there's not much they can do but accept a new time that works for everyone—you included. As Keith Webb once said, what gets scheduled gets done. And (I'll add), what gets scheduled prevents other people from scheduling over you.

> "What gets scheduled gets done. And, what gets scheduled prevents other people from scheduling over you."

The second defense is just as cut-and-dried. When you're occupied, don't answer the phone. Period. Not only is this good practice for staying in the flow. It's also a defensive maneuver for preventing interruptions that put more work on your plate than you can afford. Sure, you can set your phone in do-not-disturb mode, but I'd rather you train yourself to ignore calls when in the groove of deep work. Do-not-disturb is a nice feature, but if my mind is craving "just a peek" at my screen, I'm not really able to focus and my undisturbed time is disturbed by my cravings. Finally, if you can, send the caller a text message letting them know you're busy. This prevents them from following up with a call to your desk, a text message, and an email when you don't pick up.

The third and final defense is simple. Send out not-so-subtle signals that you're not to be disturbed. Put on headphones to indicate you're busy. Buy a cheap cone at your local sporting goods store and tape a sign to it that says "Concentrating, Do Not Disturb." Place it behind your chair for all to see.

Finally, should these defenses not work, go on the offense. When people do grab your attention (and it's too rude to tell them to shut up and leave you alone), be proactive. When they call, ask how you can help them immediately, preventing them from initiating a five-minute chit-chat about nothing useful. When they come to your door, get up and greet them so they don't have a chance to sit and blow 15 minutes shooting the shit. If you're busy, ask them to come back in a bit when you'll be free. And, when all else fails, find another place to work for a while. Leaving the office allows others to get in their own groove and stop asking for help. You can safely sneak back in later with less likelihood of interruption.

Saying "No" the Right (and Polite) Way

When all other defenses fail, and they will, it's time to say "no." But not in a nasty, I'm-never-going-to-help-you way. Many times, a perfectly reasonable request for help comes in. With a prioritized to-do list and a full calendar, you'll find it easy to say, "I'm completely slammed right now and won't be able to get to that until later." This graciously acknowledges the other persons' need for help without committing to help them immediately. If they can wait until later, great. If not, they'll find someone else to help them. Don't be surprised if they didn't come to you for any particular reason. It's possible someone else less busy can help them. Even if they can't, you haven't left them hanging. You'll just help them later.

However you say it, you'll want to make sure the person who is requesting your time understands it's not about them. It's not personal. You simply don't have time due to other commitments, obligation, and priorities.

Nobody will push you to reschedule a meeting that's already on your calendar. They know it's rude to assume their time is more valuable than yours. Treat your priorities like meetings. Schedule them, commit to them, then execute them.

If someone insists, resist. Tell them you'll look over your commitments and get back to them. If you can take on the additional commitment, great. If not, tell them when you might be able to. It might be a month from now, which might sound like a "no," and they'll likely find someone else to do it quicker.

All that said, even the most delicate "no" won't work on someone like your boss, and I don't recommend telling them "no" outright. Instead, agree to do what they ask, but ask them to help you prioritize the other important matters you're dealing with at the moment. Many times, managers will hear a new idea and get excited to implement it right away. When you show them everything on your plate, tasks that they were once excited about and committed resources to, they'll back off the new idea until you're done. They can't reasonably ask you to perform two high-priority tasks simultaneously. Asking them to help you prioritize will force them to focus your efforts on one or the other.

Whatever you do, be responsive. Get back to anyone that asks for your time. If you don't respond quickly, you're inviting interruption after interruption. If you never respond to people's requests, they will pester you via other means—sending an email before calling, texting before stopping by your office. Respond to requests within a reasonable amount of time. Immediately if possible. At your next break if not. Let them know you'll get to it, and by when. Then set a reminder for yourself and do it.

Finally, if all else fails, say what you mean and mean what you say. Tell the requestor what your priorities are. Let them know that you thought through their request, but just can't find time to fit it in between x, y, and z. Apologize, make sure they understand you listened to their request, tell them you hope to have time to help them in the future, and get back to your important work.

Pro Tip #1 — Decide as Your Future Self

Not every new project or request is created equal. To further protect your time, consider whether something new will take your time once or for days, weeks, or months on end. *Never* blindly accept a recurring or lengthy task without considering all you have to do over the next few months. Even if you don't have anything scheduled, think through what *should* be on your schedule. Then, think through what *could* be on your schedule. Then and only then can you decide whether to take on a new project or request.

Events and conferences are a good example. They often sound exciting at first, are booked in fun locations, and are scheduled far enough in advance that your calendar is not likely to be filled. As such, it's easy to register without thinking.

But how many times have you scheduled something far out only to arrive on the day and feel you'd rather not participate. That's because you have real work to do and, though this event has been sitting in your calendar for weeks or months, it's now intruding on the important tasks you need to get done.

Instead of blindly signing up for such events, think ahead to the day before. In other words, think about whether you could afford to attend if the event were happening tomorrow. Would it be important enough to interrupt your purpose, your vision, your goals, and all the other work you're doing that matters? If not, that event or request won't magically get more important in the future. Just politely decline and be happy knowing you saved your future self a few hours of lost time.

Pro Tip #2 — Polite Doesn't Mean Wishy Washy

All through high-school and college, I didn't drink. Most of it was driven by fear and lack of bad influences. But I quickly found that not drinking could be worn as a badge of honor.

It only took two parties to get good at saying, "I don't drink." While almost everyone would ask why, nobody forced the issue.

On the other hand, I witnessed many, many friends turn down a drink by saying, "not tonight," only to feel the pressure mount. Unlike the resoluteness of saying "I don't drink," saying "not tonight" is soft. It's wishy washy. It opened them up to badgering, harassment, and relentless coercion.

The same will go for your time. If you don't do meetings on Mondays, say so. If you won't travel outside the state for only one meeting, let people know. If you don't work between 5:30 pm and 8 pm so you can spend time with your kids, mention that the next time a meeting request comes in and watch how fast it gets rescheduled.

Whatever you do, don't be wishy washy. Be polite, but be resolute, and stick to your guns.

#

Our purpose, vision, and goals guide us when others' request our time and attention. Without these, we'd never have a good reason to say "no." With them, it becomes easy to understand whether we can work on a new task or project.

But you still have to say the word. You still have to make the hard choices. Just because you have time, doesn't mean you should agree to spending that time on someone else's to-do list. There's no getting home early if you can never make progress on what matters.

"We can better serve the world when we have time to respond thoughtfully instead of reacting mindlessly."

— Courtney Carver, Soulful Simplicity: How Living with Less Can Lead to So Much More

PART V

Optimize Your Time

Aligning mind, body, and environment to maximize your time and energy

"Life is long if you know how to use it." — Seneca

Chapter Fifteen

Creating New Expectations

"Treat a man as he is and he will remain as he is. Treat a man as he can and should be and he will become as he can and should be."

— Stephen R. Covey, The 7 Habits of Highly Effective People: Powerful Lessons in Personal Change

It looked like a Coke. The brown sugary liquid fizzed over a tall glass of ice just like a Coke would. My college roommate even handed it to me saying, "here's your Coke." I grabbed the glass without a thought, thanked him, took a swig and… Spit out a mouthful of the nastiest tasting liquid onto my chin and all over my shirt. It may as well have been motor oil. It tasted that bad.

I shot a look at my roommate, a combination of disgust and surprise, to tell him the Coke had spoiled. But his smirk suggested he was up to his pranks again. And this time, I was his target.

As it turned out, there was nothing wrong with the drink. It simply wasn't the drink I was expecting. I had asked my roommate to grab me a glass of Coke. He brought me a glass of root beer instead. Funny.

The thing is, I love root beer. There's nothing better than a tall glass of ice-cold Mug on a hot day. I have fond memories of pulling up to an A&W in the back of my Grandma's beige Cadillac where the waitress would hang a tray of frozen glasses full of the sweet drink on our window. But, because my brain was expecting one flavor and my taste buds delivered something completely different, it malfunctioned causing a visceral reaction that had my roommate laughing at me for hours.

Your Brain is an Expectation Machine

Everything you do, or experience, or think is affected by the expectations you already have. Take your arms, for example. With both arms intact, your brain works swimmingly. It sends signals to your limbs, they move, they provide feedback, and your brain breathes a sigh of relief that the cycle is complete. When you expect your arm to move and it does, your expectations are fulfilled. All is well. But if one arm were missing, the same feedback loop doesn't close. A variety of sensations, including pain, can follow.

In a fascinating book called "Phantoms in the Brain", Dr. Ramachandran explores the world of neuroscience through people who have lost a limb. Patients experienced phantom sensations in an extremity that no longer existed; some as simple as a fleeting tickle, others as irritating as an un-itchable itch and, in the worst of cases, pain. The patient's brain, having sent a signal to the missing limb, would expect a response. Without receiving one, its neural pathways would get confused, causing severe phantom pain where none should be possible.

Or take relationships, for example. While you may pride yourself on accepting strangers with open eyes—never judging, never assuming—how you actually treat them is, in part, based on expectations you already have for them.

In a pivotal study performed by Harvard Professor Robert Rosenthal in 1964, a random group of students was given a standardized IQ test. From the pool of test results, Rosenthal selected a few children at random and told their teachers that his test predicted children who were "on the verge of an intense intellectual bloom." Rosenthal then followed these children and their teachers for two years. What he found was astounding. The randomly chosen children, children whose teachers had higher expectations for them, now performed better on IQ tests than the other students in his study. In short, the teachers' expectations for a student could affect that students' development.

In both studies, the study of phantom pain in missing limbs and of setting high (albeit false) expectations of a student's performance, we see that our brains aren't operating how we think. We *believe* we receive stimulus through our senses, process it, then consciously decide how to react. But in reality, we receive stimulus through our senses, our brain processes it, then delivers answers based on what it *expects* to see next. Unless we interrupt our brain's processing and delivery system, we may receive answers that aren't logical, reasonable, or even appropriate. While this may seem cause for alarm, it's actually quite helpful.

Your Expectations Maximize Your Productivity

Most of the time, you're on autopilot. Wake up, make coffee, eat breakfast, shower, and head to work. You do these things without thinking. From the second your alarm goes off; your brain begins to execute a series of routines. Unless something unexpected comes up, these run without a hitch.

During the day, many other programs execute without your involvement: meeting with people, triaging emails, eating lunch, social media, and driving home all happen without much contemplation on your part. Yes, you're engaged, participating, even interacting. But you're not thinking deeply. You know what's expected of you and easily live up to those expectations. Your brain, the ultimate expectation machine, moves from one program to the next, predicting what will happen and delivering answers that match reality with your assumptions. You're doing whatever comes to mind. And that's a good thing — most of the time.

Autopilot lets you act without thinking, perform without expending energy, and make decisions without deciding. It lets you talk to a friend while driving a stick shift. It lets you shampoo your hair while mentally preparing for an upcoming meeting. With autopilot turned on, you can move through your morning routine in a sleep-deprived daze, making coffee, eating breakfast, and triaging emails using minimal mental resources.

But when it comes to focusing on that which matters, autopilot, for all its energy-saving and decision-making benefits, is hugely limiting. Even with good intentions—plans to eat right, exercise, set goals, build your side-hustle, or get home before dinner—it sometimes seems impossibly difficult get things done. We all have our reasons: There's too much to do. Too little time. Too many distractions. Too many competing priorities. Too many things to remember. And, life just seems to get in the way.

These reasons sound well and good, but (truth bomb coming) they're all lies. The real reason you don't eat right, exercise, set goals, grow your business, and live a balanced life isn't because you have too much to do. It's not because you get distracted. It's because you aren't conditioned to.

If you always eat breakfast after making coffee, your autopilot switches you from coffee-mode to breakfast-mode without thinking. If your morning routine has never included exercise, inserting a workout is jarring. Even now, having developed a plan from purpose through goals, it's not going to be easy to meet those goals, live your vision, and realize your purpose. In some ways, your brain rejects the necessary changes, making it far easier to fall back into a familiar routine. A routine that's safe. A routine you're comfortable with.

Achieving your goals requires change. Living a new vision for your life requires change. It requires us to do things we're not familiar with, that we're uncomfortable with. But our routines, the expectations we've built for how our life runs, they don't allow for the uncomfortable. They don't allow for interruptions. And they don't allow for growth. As such, without modifying your expectations, you can't hope to change. And without change, you can't hope to grow.

"The measure of intelligence is the ability to change."

— Albert Einstein

Why Self-Improvement is So Effing Hard

If you expect to drink a Coke and your prankster roommate gives you a root beer instead, your brain cries foul. Not because you don't like root beer, but because you're geared up to taste Coke and your brain tells you something is wrong. Similarly, if you introduce exercise in your morning routine when you're used to eating breakfast after making coffee, your brain will initially cry foul. It won't feel right. It won't be expected. And that's when the excuses come. "I just don't have enough time to exercise. Not this morning."

If you lost a limb in an unfortunate accident, your brain might feel confused. Similarly, if you try reading a productivity book after breakfast when you would normally read the news, your brain will feel the same. You'll worry that you're missing out on important world events. A mild form of pain will crop up. And that's when the excuses come. "There are just too many other important things to read. I'll read this book tomorrow."

Or, as we learned with Professor Rosenthal's teaching experiment, the expectations we set for others changes the way we interact with them. If you're used to doing everything yourself but know a mentor could help accelerate your business, the expectation you have for yourself (an expectation that you can do it all) will prevent you from finding that new mentor. That's when the excuses come. "Finding a mentor just isn't a priority right now. I'll look for one next week."

#

You have to break out of autopilot. And the good news is, you can. You don't have to live a life of conditioned response, doing whatever your brain is expecting. You can improve. You can grow. You can break through self-imposed barriers that cause fear, uncertainty, and doubt.

Breaking your expectations won't happen overnight. As we've already seen, habits take a minimum of 66 days to form. You're literally reprogramming your brain to create new expectations. You're telling your brain that the habits and routines it's already familiar with should be replaced by something else. Something hard. Something uncomfortable. Something that forces you to grow.

But, if you practice using the scientifically proven productivity techniques learned so far, in a little over two months, these changes will be routine, and you'll be able to change more. The productivity benefits will compound over time.

Understand that productivity is not a matter of willpower. Many aspects of it lie outside our ability to control. However, using a few neuroscience concepts to our advantage, we can create new expectations and habits that set us on a path to success, profoundly altering our life for the better. And, it all starts in the mind.

Chapter Sixteen

The Productive Mind

"I am, indeed, a king, because I know how to rule myself."

— Pietro Aretino

Since entering the workforce, I've lived on the East coast while working for West coast companies. When I first started, I was 24 years old, flying to San Francisco and home every six weeks. I worked in a small office with a small team where everyone knew everyone. Most of us were young. Our leadership team wasn't much older.

The flight west to San Francisco was always easy. Leave in the morning, fly five hours, land in the morning two hours later (thanks to the time shift). It was the flight home that was hell. Feeling like I had something to prove, I'd take the red-eye after a full day of work instead of waiting until morning to return home—11 pm to 6:30 am. With the time shift, it was only 4 hours of sleep, if I was lucky.

Glutton for punishment or eager to please the elders, I'd land from that red eye, grab a shower, eat breakfast, and head into the office.

Everyone wanted to know about my flight and was keen on doling out admiration for my dedication to the job.

"You must be tired," they'd say.

"I'll sleep when I die," I'd respond.

Over the years, I'd use that phrase repeatedly. "I'll sleep when I die" got around, and I'd hear others (and myself) wearing it as a badge of honor.

Work, work, work, I thought. Push, push, push. There are projects to be done, tasks to complete, and no time for leisurely flights home or morning naps after a red eye.

But, the fact of the matter is, those days after a red eye were my most unproductive days of all. I'd get a few things done in the morning and hit a big fat lull. Neither coffee nor meditation nor fresh air could snap me out of it. Many times, I'd doze off with my eyes open, staring at my computer screen, pretending as if I was working but really just fighting the need for shut eye.

I was fooling myself. I was telling myself that I had so much to prove, so much work to do, that I couldn't rest and take care of myself. I was lying to myself that I was getting more done feeling like a zombie than if I'd just gone home, recovered, and started fresh the day after.

Productivity starts in the mind. And it starts with a good night's sleep.

Sleep and Productivity

Beyond the negative health effects of not getting enough sleep, a lack of shut eye directly and adversely impacts productivity in more ways than one. In the worst circumstances, sleep deprivation can cause mental errors resulting in lost lives.

For example, sleep deprived surgeons are 20-30% more likely to commit errors than those with enough sleep ("Productivity and sleep," 2020). The 1979 nuclear disaster at Three Mile Island and the 1986 nuclear episode at Chernobyl both cited sleep deprivation as a major contributing factor. Similarly, the Challenger space shuttle disaster and the Exxon Valdez oil tanker spill were both found to have been caused by, in major part, sleep deprivation ("Sleep, Performance," 2007). While those are drastic examples, they point out how important sleep can be, specifically on our ability to focus.

If you could focus 100% on the task at hand, productivity would be no issue. But distractions inevitably crop up, and sleep deprivation makes it difficult to refocus once preoccupied. Your brains attention center can't regain control and you may find yourself lost to whatever new, shiny object is dangling in front of you.

Furthermore, lack of sleep is linked to procrastination and negative mood. Without enough sleep, you'll tire 11% faster making all the difference toward the end of your workday (Hindy, n.d.). Which is just about the worst time to be tired. The end of the workday is when you're wrapping everything up. It's when you're trying to plow through those final tasks so you can get outta dodge. With enough sleep, you'll finish the day strong. Without, you'll struggle to get that last bit of work done. You'll feel slow and lethargic, as if drunk.

In fact, after working 17 to 19 hours, your brain works about as well as it does after a few glasses of wine. After 24 hours, your brain acts as if it has a blood-alcohol concentration of 0.10. You can't legally drive under that spell in all 50 states (Hindy, n.d.). How will you get real work done?

If it's not clear by now, the key to getting more productive isn't sleeping less, it's sleeping more. But it's also sleeping more regularly.

In a study that compared sleep schedules of Harvard college students for a month, participants who held a regular sleep schedule earned better GPAs than those who didn't. Even though both sets of students got a similar amount of sleep each night, those who held irregular sleeping patterns would find themselves in a state of jet lag as melatonin was released at irregular times in their body ("Productivity and sleep," 2020).

"The secret to becoming more productive is not managing your time; it's managing your energy."

— Michael Hyatt

So sleep is important. How do you get enough of it? Many sleep experts, including the National Sleep Foundation, suggest a minimum of six hours and recommend between seven and nine. Of course, needs vary from one person to the next. Finding out how much sleep you need is stupid simple: If you need an alarm to wake up, you probably haven't gotten enough.

Waking up without an alarm requires one simple adjustment to your day: Go to bed earlier. You don't have to do it all at once. Just go to bed 15 minutes earlier every night until you wake up before your alarm. Take note of how many hours you slept. After a week or two, you'll have built up a good feeling for how much you need. If you absolutely need to wake up at a certain time, you can always set a drop-dead wake-up alarm. But with a handle on how much sleep you need, you may not even need it. And the beauty of waking up without an alarm is you can't hit the snooze button—a button that contributes to feelings of fatigue hours after waking.

In a study of nearly 20,000 people, less than 10% woke up without an alarm while over 50% hit the snooze button. In many cases multiple times (Helmer, 2019). Those that hit the snooze button felt more fatigued throughout the day. If you've felt like napping at your desk the middle of the day for no damn reason, your snooze button may have been the cause.

Not that napping in the afternoon is bad. Even with a good night's sleep, waking up without an alarm and avoiding the snooze button, most of us notice a post-lunch lull. That's because, like 88 percent of non-human mammals that nap during daylight hours, your natural body clock is primed to grab a period of deep sleep at night between 2 am and 4 am, and then again from 1 pm to 3 pm in the afternoon. Most of us have the night sleeping session locked down. It's that afternoon "ciesta" that's frowned upon, at least in the US. But with NASA showing that a nap can increase performance by 34% and alertness by 100%, and with the National Sleep Foundation suggesting a short nap can "[improve] alertness and performance without leaving you feeling groggy or interfering with nighttime sleep", maybe it's time to consider shutting down around 2 pm like many famous historical figures have been doing for hundreds of years (Jager, 2019).

Leonardo da Vinci, Napoleon, Albert Einstein, Thomas Edison, Eleanor Roosevelt, John F. Kennedy, Rockefeller, Churchill, Lyndon B. Johnson, and Ronald Reagan all took daily naps. Some in addition to getting plenty of sleep at night (Hyatt, 2016). And, while it's impossible to correlate their napping with their success, you can't say that any of these legends weren't wildly accomplished.

> "Nature has not intended mankind to work from eight in the morning until midnight without refreshment of blessed oblivion which, even if it only lasts twenty minutes, is sufficient to renew all the vital forces."
>
> —Winston Churchill

In short, if you need to restore energy in the afternoon, a brief 20 to 30-minute nap can do the trick. Just take care not to sleep too much. Anything longer than 30 minutes puts you into stage three sleep, a deeper sleep that, if broken, will leave you feeling groggy and more tired than when you drifted off (Hyatt, 2016).

Side Note: How do you take a long enough nap without falling into a deep sleep? Try resting with some loose change or your car keys in your hand over the floor. When you finally doze off, but before you hit a deep slumber, you'll drop the keys and wake yourself up. Perfect.

I hope by now the point is clear. You must make sleep a priority. You can't think, "oh well, I'll get to bed when I get to bed and, if I get to bed late, I just deal with it tomorrow." That's not making sleep a priority. That's putting sleep in the back seat.

Making sleep a priority means thinking about when you need to wake up and giving yourself ample time to wind down at night. It means getting to bed early enough that you can get that seven to nine hours necessary to wake up without an alarm, feel refreshed, and carry out a productive day. Making sleep a priority means planning some time after lunch to get 20 minutes of shut eye, recharging yourself such that you can have a focused and productive afternoon. Making sleep a priority means using the planning and scheduling tools we learned in Chapter Eleven to literally plan it into your schedule and day.

Anything else isn't prioritizing sleep. It's letting the demands and distractions of the world drive your day. And that's something to meditate on.

Meditation and Productivity

I'll admit, my history with meditation has been hot and cold. I often hear the benefits of meditation, get inspired to try it, then fall back into other sources of introspective solitude like journaling, online shopping, or watching cat videos. But the scientifically studied benefits of meditation are too hard to ignore. Especially in a book like this. So, like the other chapters in this book, I set out to do some research. I just didn't find the results you'd expect.

There are thousands upon thousands of articles claiming multiple benefits of meditation including stress reduction, controlled anxiety, improved emotional health, increased attention span, and improved sleep. Meditation has become the favorite stepchild of all the life-hacks, often cited by highly followed podcasters and Instagram celebrities as something we all should do to immediately improve our quality of life. But the studies on meditation researching these particular benefits have mixed reviews.

For example, one study by the Greater Los Angeles VA Healthcare System found improved sleep benefits of mindfulness-based stress reduction and mindfulness-based therapy while another study by multiple medicinal and psychological departments at Johns Hopkins University in Baltimore, MD found "low evidence of no effect or insufficient evidence of any effect of meditation programs on positive mood, attention, substance use, eating habits, sleep, and weight." Their findings also found no evidence that meditation was better than medicine, working out, or more typical physical, psychological, or behavioral therapies (Goyal, Singh, Sibinga, Gould, Rowland-Seymour, Sharma, Berger, Sleicher, Maron, Shihab, Ranasinghe, Linn, Saha, Bass, & Haythornthwaite, 2014). Yet another study by Michael Mrazek, Michael Franklin, Dawa Phillips, Benjamin Baird, and Johnathan Schooler (2013) at the Department of Psychological and Brain Sciences at the University of California, Santa Barbara found measurable benefits meditation had on reducing mind-wandering and improving working memory of GRE test participants.

One study says one thing. Another says another. It's exactly what my history with meditation looks like—confusing.

As early as high-school, I was studying Zen Buddhism and martial arts books, all of which had healthy doses of meditative inspiration. I'd find a quiet spot in the house and practice meditation techniques of the ancient samurai and Shaolin monks. However, after a few months of this, and without any tracked data to show whether I was improving my life in any meaningful way, I'd give up. Later I'd hear about meditation benefits on a podcast or an Internet article, which would inspire me to try it again. Fast forward a few weeks and I'd be right back to my normal morning routine, leaving meditation for only those times when I felt particularly scatter-brained and needed to calm my thoughts.

Unfortunately, I cannot cite a specific scientific research paper claiming productivity benefits of meditation without also citing research papers that deny those benefits. As such, I must leave the results of meditation completely in your hands.

Try meditation. Try it consistently for a few weeks. Search online for any one of a thousand meditation techniques and sit for a few minutes daily in meditative practice.

When I do meditate, I like simply clearing my mind, focusing on my breath, and gently dismissing any thoughts that come to mind. Alone with my thoughts, a candle, and the darkness of the morning makes for, at the very least, a gentle way to wake up. At best, it may very reduce my stress, increase my focus, and positively affecting my productivity in unknown ways.

If, after trying meditation, you find it's not your thing, try mindfulness. Where meditation is a quiet, personal exercise limiting distractions while focusing on your breath, mindfulness is something you can practice anywhere. It requires only that you be present— present to every sensation from all five senses. Notice what you are seeing, what you are hearing, what you are feeling. The feeling of the chair against your back, the smell of the room you're in, the taste of food in your mouth.

Mindfulness is especially powerful when practiced while communicating. Focusing 100% on the other party without allowing your environment (ahem, your phone) to distract you increases your ability to concentrate and is the basis of a lasting relationship.

After trying either meditation or mindfulness for a bit, take note of how it affects your ability to focus, concentrate, and get your most important work done. If it helps, incorporate it into the system you're building here. If it doesn't, drop it like it's hot.

Caffeine and Productivity

I got my coffee drinking addiction from my parents. They're a two-pot-a-day kind of couple, easily killing eight hot cups in the morning brewed strong. As a joke, my Fathers' colleagues once bought him a 64-ounce coffee mug, enough to hold an entire pot of coffee in it at once. He kept it on his desk with candies, pens, and other office trinkets, but I knew he secretly wanted to fill it and chug it like a boss.

My addiction to coffee started slow. I'd brew a pot in college when family visited, carrying around a cup to feel like one of the grown-ups. Soon after graduating, I joined a software engineering company where coffee was borderline worshipped. They would double the coffee grounds in a doubled-up filter, making sure the water soaked long enough to hit maximum saturation by the little brown beans. If I didn't know better, I'd have thought they were brewing something illegal. We all drank it like it was.

We thought we were keeping ourselves awake, productive, focused. As it turns out, we were wrong.

We believe caffeine wakes us up. If that were the case, then keeping our cups full all day as if drip feeding it through an IV into our bloodstream would be a good idea. But, while caffeine does give you a momentary (albeit short lived) boost of energy, its main effect isn't that it wakes you up. It's that it prevents you from feeling tired in the first place.

Sleepiness is felt when a naturally produced brain-chemical, adenosine, binds to receptors in the brain. The longer you're awake, the more adenosine builds up. By the time night hits, the buildup is enough to prepare it for sleep. While you can push through this feeling to pull an all-nighter or two, eventually you'll have so much adenosine in your brain that you'll fall asleep against your will. We can use caffeine to prevent this from happening, to an extent.

Caffeine's unique ability is to bind to the same adenosine receptors in the brain. Once bound, adenosine can't bind to those same receptors. As a result, your brain receptors are like a Costco parking lot on Black Friday, completely full of caffeine. The adenosine drives around looking for a parking spot, but can't find one. It can't park, so you don't feel sleepy.

Of course, this effect doesn't last forever. Caffeine has a half-life of five to six hours, so over time, a parking spot will finally open up. The adenosine will rebind with your brain and push you into a sleepy state. If you re-caffeinate before this happens, you'll stay alert a while longer. The problem is, your brain will continue to produce adenosine with no place to park, leaving it all floating around. And, just like you'd feel driving around the Costco parking lot for hours and never finding a spot, all those adenosine's floating around will get really fucking huffy, giving you a terrible headache, fogginess, or that feeling you got hit by bus.

Knowing all this, we can and should change our coffee-drinking habits. Instead of slugging down cup after cup, we can implement a more intelligent strategy.

Drink caffeine to give you that initial boost when you wake up if you need it (which you shouldn't if you're getting enough sleep—see Chapter Sixteen). But, if you can, hold off for a while. Wait until right before those adenosine chemicals start infiltrating your brain. Don't feed your caffeine addiction until after you've had some time to wake up, after you get going with your day, and before the adenosine mounts its attack.

Remember, caffeine isn't giving you energy, it's preventing you from getting sleepy. As such, it makes sense to wait for two or three hours before caffeinating. This will keep your productivity going well through the morning and into the early afternoon, when you might consider caffeinating again before that post-lunch food coma.

Of course, if you already feel sleepy, it's too late. That's okay. Drink a full cup of coffee before taking a short nap (again, see Chapter Sixteen where we discuss the benefits of napping). While the caffeine is absorbing into your bloodstream and traveling to your brain, your brain is resetting itself and removing the adenosine build-up. The caffeine finds a parking spot and, when you wake up, has taken over to push the sleepiness out.

Just be careful not to drink caffeine too late in the day. As I mentioned earlier, caffeine has a half-life of five to six hours. That means, having a cup of coffee after a 6 pm dinner means a full half of the caffeine you consumed is still attached to the receptors in your brain at 11 or 12 at night. Try cutting yourself off at least 10 hours before bedtime to give yourself the best chance of sleeping soundly, feeling refreshed the next morning, and preventing that horrible headache filled grogginess that comes with drinking too much, too often, and too late in the day.

Chapter Seventeen

The Productive Body

"Amateurs sit and wait for inspiration, the rest of us just get up and go to work."

— Stephen King, On Writing: A Memoir of the Craft

G iven enough sleep, solitude, and caffeine, we feel as though we can accomplish anything. Yet, a functioning but unhealthy body has been shown to be considerably less productive (Foodtolive, 2017).

We all know what unhealthy looks like. Bad food, little exercise, and high stress levels. These things contribute to an overall unwellness that affects how much work we can get done on any given day. Given that, it's no surprise that good food, exercise, and low stress levels lead to a higher state of well-being. The question becomes, *how much* does our nutrition, fitness, and stress level affect what we get done, and how does optimizing all three increase our ability to get things done?

Exercise and Productivity

For as complicated a machine as your brain is, it's also actually quite simple. Sitting on the couch leaves it inactive, resting, conserving energy. Begin running, moving around weights, or performing any other strenuous activity and you fool your brain into thinking you're in danger, activating fight or flight mode.

It's nothing to be concerned about, and you won't feel the panic you'd feel while being chased by a rabid tiger. Rather, your brain simply releases the protein BDNF or Brain Derived Neurotrophic Factor, which simultaneously repairs your neurons, in effect, resetting your brain. At the same time, endorphins are released to block some of the pain associated with physical activity, making you more comfortable while working out (Widrich, 2014).

Perhaps this is why, in a study of 200 workers presented at the American College of Sports Medicine in Nashville, Tennessee, researchers found that on-the-job performance increased by up to 15 percent with 30 to 60 minutes of exercise per day. Sixty percent of those workers said they experienced increases in mental performance, time management, and meeting deadlines on these exercise days (Drannan, n.d.).

That's not the only evidence showing how exercise increases productivity. A Briston University study of 200 employees showed that people rated their concentration 22% higher, were 22% more likely to finish their work on time, were 25% more productive without breaks, and were 41% more motivated to work on days when they exercised vs. days they did not ("How to Increase Your Productivity," n.d.). In yet another study performed in a large Southern California company, two groups were measured by the University of La Verne, Aghop Der-Karabeitian and Norma Gebharbp on the basis of job satisfaction, body image, and sick days. One group spent six months in a physical fitness program, the other group did not. The physical fitness group reported higher job satisfaction, better body image, and reported fewer sick days than the control group (Sharifzadeh, 2013). Finally, one last study measured commercial real estate brokers who did 12 weeks of aerobic exercises vs. their counterparts who didn't participate. The results for the active agents? You guessed it. Higher sales output (Sharifzadeh, 2013).

Higher concentration, more likely to finish work, less likely to take breaks, more motivated, higher job satisfaction, better body image, fewer sick days, and more sales. All compelling reasons to get fit. And they all make sense.

Working out increases blood flow through your entire body. While you're working out, you're taking in more oxygen. The combined effect of greater oxygen and blood to your brain naturally increases focus and mental clarity. That, plus the longer term benefits such as reduced body weight, reduced risk for medical conditions, improved cardiovascular health, improved immunity, and reduced risk for obesity and type two diabetes are important effects that will keep you productive now *and* prevent you from losing productivity via hospital visits and sick days as you age.

> "Time and health are two precious assets that we don't recognize and appreciate until they have been depleted."
>
> – Denis Waitley

Given these studies, you might think that the more you exercise, the more productive you will be. This is quite the opposite.

When it comes to length and vigor, a low-intensity workout is more effective than a high-intensity one for reducing fatigue and avoiding the decline of attention, memory, and problem solving ("How to Increase Your Productivity," n.d.). And, while the American College of Sports recommends a minimum of 10 minutes for an energy boost, somewhere between 20 and 30 minutes of low-intensity exercise seems to be optimal for sustained output throughout the day (Tate, 2015).

A light jog, bike ride, elliptical, or other similar activity gives you an immediate energy boost by releasing serotonin, which helps you feel better and improves your mood better than anything besides sex. It also increases the number of mitochondria in your cells. Since mitochondria produce ATP, a chemical your body and brain use for energy, the more you work out, the more energy you will have over time. In short, working out makes you feel immediately better, then later has your cells producing more energy daily. In a matter of weeks, you may start seeing impactful effects (Pozen, 2012).

Twenty to thirty minutes in the morning is just enough to provide an immediate energy boost, kill that groggy feeling, and crush the rest of your day. And, as an alternative to a nap, it's possible to use a similar amount of low-intensity exercise to lift your mood once that mid-afternoon slump hits.

While all of this information about exercise comes from countless studies, I've long believed that exercise is only partially about physical fitness. It's also about your mind.

When you exercise, you have the chance to make your mind a slave to your will. If you can push through mental barriers and separate yourself from discomfort in your body, you can do the same thing during the workday.

At the very least, exercise puts structure in your day. It can help break a slump. It can recharge your creativity when the juices stop flowing. Over time, a regular exercise routine becomes the foundation on which all other activities are built.

Nutrition and Productivity

The foods we eat have a direct impact on our health, which, in turn, has a direct impact on our ability to get things done. Ironically, in an effort to give ourselves more working hours by eating packaged and processed foods, we are not only hurting our health, we may be wasting our time and money.

The British Journal of Health Psychology website links fatigue decreased mental effectiveness, and workplace performance to poor nutrition (Dickinson, 2017). This may be due to the change in mood caused by poor dietary choices. Irritability, stress, depression, and decreased energy levels can all play a role when the brain and body aren't nourished properly. This can come from something as simple as eating processed foods. Saturated fats, often found in processed (or junk) food, have shown negative effects on test subjects. In a 2008 study of how breakfast affected test scores in school children, researchers found that children who ate fast food three times a week had lower test scores of up to 16% ("What's in the Breakroom," 2009).

As it turns out, saturated fats aren't the only thing that can affect our ability to concentrate and perform. With a measly 1% drop in hydration, water can decrease your productivity levels by upwards of 20%. An iron deficiency has been shown to impair physical work by 30%. In a 2007 study of 149 test subjects, 42 had sufficient iron levels and outperformed the other 107 subjects in cognitive tests. After 16 weeks of receiving proper levels of iron, previously underperformed test subjects saw a 500% to 700% increase in their performance ("What's in the Breakroom," 2009).

I don't know what an iron deficiency feels like. Hell, I don't even know what proper levels of iron mean. That's between you and your doctor. But I do know that getting "hangry" is a thang, because it happens to my kids nearly every day. When their blood glucose gets low, grumpiness hits, and they become real irritable. You and I are no different. Irritability is followed by bad decision making.

In a study performed on judge's ruling on cases throughout the day, researchers found that "favorable rulings dropped gradually from around 65% to nearly zero with each decision session and returns abruptly to ~65% after a [food] break" (DeMers, 2017). Making an important decision in your life or at work? Maybe make sure you're well fed first.

And when I say well fed, I mean eat whole, healthy food. High-glucose foods like white bread and candy may give you an immediate energy and alertness boost, but the crash will leave you feeling drowsy, weak, and unable to perform optimally. It's better to fill your belly with lower glycemic index foods such as fruits, veggies, and whole grains which steadily release energy for hours. Just make sure you don't fill yourself with too much of it. Foods high in calories cause an energy tax on our digestive system diverting blood and oxygen to our gut, depriving us from that same blood and oxygen to our brains. The same effects occur: sluggishness, and an overall decrease in performance ("Nutrition and Productivity," 2017).

That's a lot to take in. But it's important. Though our brain only accounts for 2% of our body's total weight, it consumes 20% of our body's total energy ("Nutrition and Productivity," 2017). How we fuel that energy hog can make a huge difference in how we go about our day. If done right—eating healthy and getting enough water, protein, iron, and vitamins—Perspectives in Public Health, a journal on health and nutrition, says that we can increase our overall productivity by at least 2% (Dickinson, 2017). While that doesn't sound like much, it's an extra 50 minutes of free time at the end of a workweek.

Stress and Productivity

Bottom line up front? Stress is not a bad word. Stress, in measured doses, is actually good for productivity.

We often think of stress in a bad light. And for good reason. Too much stress on a bridge can cause it to collapse. Too much stress on a baseball bat can cause it to shatter. Too much stress on a human can cause them to get really fucking grumpy. On the flip side, too little stress results in an inactive lifestyle. You might recognize such a person as lacking drive or being too laid back; they just don't seem to care about getting anything done and are under no pressure to produce results.

In reality, stress sits on a continuum starting with too little (where you are an inactive couch-sloth) and ending with too much (where you burnout). The right balance is managing your stress level to an optimum amount, right up to when you feel fatigue but before exhaustion sets in. This is best illustrated in the Yerkes-Dodson law chart below:

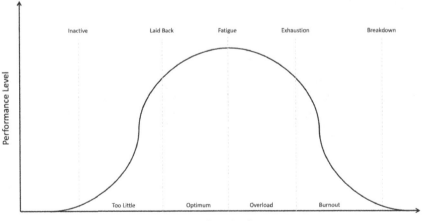

In 1908, psychologists Robert Yerkes and John Dodson set out to test the effects of stress on rats in a maze by, get this, shocking the shit out of them. When the rats were left to find their way out of the maze on their own, they managed, though it wasn't an inspired performance. When the rats were given a mild shock, low enough to stimulate and motivate them, they performed better yet. When the shock was too strong, the rats panicked. They dodged around randomly trying anything and everything to escape. In short, certain level of stress increased their performance while too much destroyed it and eventually resulted in a panic-induced breakdown (Cherry, 2020).

I've felt like a rat in a maze occasionally. Like the time I realized I wasn't prepared for an important presentation in front of 300 people. That presentation didn't go well. I rambled, meandered, and told random stories in search of my point. The audience was lost. They probably wondered if someone had wired a car battery to my head.

I choked, and I knew it. But you probably know that feeling too. Even if you haven't yourself, seen others choke when the stress mounts. Like during a football game when the kicker shanks a 20-yard game-winning kick. Or when professional players collide in the outfield over a routine pop fly during the final game in the World Series.

Think of stress like a cup of water. Every time you feel the pressure to perform, a bit of water goes into the glass. High pressure means more water. If you don't take the time to pour some water out (by relaxing, sleeping, or otherwise recharging), the glass will eventually overflow, and you'll end up feeling like a shocked rat in a maze. You'll know you overdid it if you feel some of the psychological and physiological symptoms of stress—tension, headaches, boredom, ulcers, high blood pressure, and lack of appetite to name a few (Subbulaxmi, n.d.).

When it comes to performing your job to maximum productivity without choking or burning out, the stress can't be too high. You need to find that yellow zone; lower than overwhelmed but higher than laid back. If you can find a way to live in this zone, you'll be working at maximum productivity. Of course, as we explored in the second myth of productivity in Chapter Two, you can't operate at maximum productivity forever. At least, not without rest and relaxation.

To alleviate stress, take time for yourself. To prevent it from accumulating to begin with, start by being more prepared. The more you prepare for a stressful event, the more your brain will expect things to go the way you practiced. The neural pathways in your brain will carved into deep grooves making it difficult to get off track.

Once prepared, do what you can to exercise control over your environment. Any changes you can make to your digital or physical surroundings, changes that positively affect your ability to get your job done, will go a long way toward reducing stress and making the entire work experience more comfortable for you.

Finally, if you find yourself stressing out about similar tasks day after day, create a routine you can follow to prepare you for the task itself. Like a basketball player who dribbles the ball the same number of times in the same way before every free throw, you can create a routine to kick off your otherwise stressful task with an expected rhythm (Gino, 2016).

If, on the other hand, you are looking to increase your stress level and find that optimal performance zone, try taking on more responsibilities, increasing the challenge of the tasks you are performing, or setting tight deadlines for yourself. If you are struggling to hold yourself accountable, finding's an accountability partner who can take you to task if you don't do what you promised. They can help increase your stress level just enough, motivating you to get started and finish what you're working on.

Chapter Eighteen

The Productive Environment

"When a flower doesn't bloom, you fix the environment in which it grows, not the flower."

— Alexander Den Heijer

In Star Wars Episode I - The Phantom Menace, as Qui-Gon Jinn and Anakin Skywalker enter into the atmosphere of Coruscant, you can foresee the future of Earth. Qui-Gon describes the Coruscant as "... one big city," which Anakin accepts without question, as if such a planet is something any traveler would happen upon on occasion.

The path to a Coruscant-like Earth, where every square inch of land is covered by cityscape, is easy to envision. Build more roads, construct more skyscrapers, extend our infrastructures beyond their current limits. Expand upwards and outwards until the edges of our cities touch and the only patch of green remaining is Central Park in New York City—a monument to slower, less advanced times. To some extent, our lives are already like this.

179

We awake in a room closed off from the outside world, stepping into another room to make coffee and eat breakfast. We briefly enjoy the presence of Mother Nature between the front door and our car, but only if we take time to glance up as we sort through emails and texts on our phone. Arriving at work, we leave our cars, walk into square office buildings (face in phone again), sit down in square cubicles, and stare at square monitors showing square virtual windows in which we work. In other words, we're not Swiss Family Robinson. Elaborate tree houses surrounded by greenery in the deep forest are a relic of our ancestors.

By and large, I'm okay with that. I like my phone too much. And my computer and I have a 25+ year relationship that can't be broken. But current research suggests, if we're headed toward a plant-free future, we are doomed to live stressful, unhealthy, unproductive lives. Which just goes to show that our environment has a massive effect on how productive we are and can be.

> "Most people's environment is like a rushing river, going the opposite direction of where they want to go. It takes a lot of willpower to tread upstream. It's exhausting. Instead, you want your environment to pull you in the direction you want to go."
>
> — Benjamin Hardy

Preparing a Successful Environment

When you set an expectation for success, your brain rewards you with a hit of dopamine, which we learned in Chapter Three is the brain's "happy drug." Follow through on that expectation and your brain rewards you again. Knowing this, and with a bit of preparation, you can arrange your environment for a more successful outcome.

For example, if exercising is important to your daily self-improvement ritual, set an expectation that you'll succeed by laying your clothing out the night before. Not just a shirt and shorts. Arrange *everything* you need for the gym: socks, shoes, keys, wallet, water bottle (filled), gym pass, maybe even a note to yourself on why it's important to you to workout. This prep subtly tells your brain that you expect to exercise. Upon waking up, everything is ready for you. *Not* going to the gym will go against those expectations. It won't feel right. So you'll be more likely to go.

Similarly, if you know that planning your day will improve your ability to hit your goals (it will), set out your pen and planner the night before. Put a candle and lighter next to it. Have your chair pulled out and ready for you to sit in. Prep the coffee and set out your favorite mug. Sounds inviting, doesn't it? By building the perfect environment, you'll be far more likely to sit down, start planning, and actually enjoy it. Your brain won't be able to ignore the expectation you've set for yourself. You'll have created the beginnings of an environment where success is the only outcome. The rest comes down to surrounding yourself with sights, smells, and sounds, that encourage such an outcome.

> "The secret to happy workplaces isn't spending more money. It's about creating the conditions that allow employees to do their best work."
>
> — Ron Friedman, The Best Place to Work: The Art and Science of Creating an Extraordinary Workplace

Seek Novelty

When you're concentrating on, say, writing a book, having kids scream around the house on hoverboards while shooting you with Nerf darts isn't the best way to get things done. Believe me. But a coffee shop, with muted colors, stimulating smells, and a cacophony of unobtrusive background noises helps mask distractions and keep you focus on the task at hand. More so, humanities' desire to seek out new and exciting sights, sounds, and experiences is all wrapped up in one location.

As Dr Marvin Zuckerman points out in his paper entitled Desperately Seeking Sensation: Fear, Reward, and the Human Need for Novelty, we're the only species that has, at great risk to our very existence, migrated over the entire planet. Every new place we visit is interesting in all the ways the places we've already visited aren't.

We seek new experiences. We're simply wired for it. And, a coffee shop is the perfect new experience.

Plants, good smells, background music, and an attractive environment all contribute to your productivity in a coffee shop. Combined, they create a powerful environment for staying hyper-focused and getting a ton of work done in a short amount of time. The icing on the cake, as we've just learned, is that, once we enter, our brain releases our friend dopamine, giving us a small "thank you" for finding someplace new in which to work. We see tasks and projects from a new perspective. We break all the old ruts we've burned into our mind while working day after day in the same office. This gives us fresh black powder for explosive action.

> "When you're stuck on something creatively, you can't solve a problem, you go to a coffee shop."
>
> — Eric Weiner

Your Most Productive Surroundings

Your surroundings play a critical role in how you perform. Simple indoor plants are known to have multiple positive effects on air quality, stress, mental fatigue, illness, and productivity. Take, for example, the 2010 study by the University of Technology in Sydney. It showed that the presence of indoor plants resulted in large, statistically significant reductions in anxiety, depressive mood, feelings of anger, levels of fatigue, confusion, and vigor by up to 60% (McMahon, 2010).

This may be the result of cleaner air, which has been shown to increase cardiovascular health and clear thinking. Washington State University showed that increased oxygen and decreased CO_2 helped increase air moisture. While that doesn't sound like a big deal, more moisture in the air leads to healthier and more comfortable relative humidity, and reduces air pollutants such as ozone, toluene, and benzene. It also reduces high-frequency sounds and overall noise in rooms. All of this contributes to feelings of well-being and, in these studies, a 12% increase in productivity (Lohr, 2010).

The good news is, these benefits can be realized without installing an indoor jungle in your office. Just one indoor plant in a room carried many of these effects. As for which plant, NASA has studied common indoor plants in order to best understand how to remove airborne chemicals in the international space station. Common, hard-to-kill indoor plants like the Peace Lily, snake plants, devils' envy, spider plants, dracaena, aglaonema, ficus benjamin's, zamioculcas zamiifolia, and philodendron are all great choices and require little maintenance (Hill, 2017). I only wish plants could remove bad smells.

The Stink of Productivity

I can't think of a worse smell than a meatball sub at a gas station. It reminds me of dog food soaked in toilet water. Gross, I know.

Once, while traveling, I stopped at a sub shop/gas station combo and, given the lack of options in this particular city, was forced to order lunch there. With a bit of time before my meeting, I had planned to eat lunch while getting some work done. The smell made it nearly impossible.

As it turns out, problem solving while exposed to bad smells is more difficult than while exposed to smells you find pleasantly distracting. Trying to work in a "stinky situation" increases your likelihood of frustration. On the flip side, pleasant smells cause people to work more efficiently, set higher goals for themselves, and improve performance on certain tasks (Herz, 2002).

Of all the senses, smell is the strongest and influences brain activity the most. Your sense of smell is directly connected to parts of your brain that influence memory and manage emotions, intricately connecting smell with your history of experiences. Since you can't turn smell off, every experience you've ever had in which smell played a powerful role is embedded in your memory. If you had a bad childhood experience while your mom was baking bread, walking past the bakery may trigger memories of that event. Over time, you might even come to find this smell off-putting (Bradford & Desrochers, 2009).

Which is why a pleasant smell for one person might be horrible to another. I love the smell of coffee beans or a deep, oaky, red wine. My son, on the other hand, makes a gnarly face and veers away. That same son loves the smell of any sub shop, while I feel like barfing at the gas-station ones.

Smells can make or break your productivity in any environment. In what researchers refer to as "high demanding environments" such as a meeting rooms, low-arousing scents have a less distracting effect on its inhabitants and, as such, promote the productivity of the workers. Strong, colorful scents, on the other hand, may be just what the doctor ordered if you're looking to get some creative work done.

Lemon, lavender, jasmine, rosemary, cinnamon, and peppermint have been shown to boost productivity, concentration, and mood across the board. One study by Japans largest fragrance producer, the Takasago Corporation, found that typists' accuracy could be increased significantly with some scents. Those who smelled lavender made 20% fewer typing errors, 33% fewer with jasmine, and 54% fewer with lemon (Moody, n.d.).

Other scent studies have shown equally interesting and powerful results. One performed at the University of Cincinnati showed that peppermint or muguet could increase perception on a task requiring long-term attention over prolonged periods of time (Warm & Parasuraman, n.d.). Another performed at the University of Northumbria found that peppermint enhanced memory, increased cognitive processing speed, and increased alertness (Moss et al, 2008).

Cinnamon has been shown to improve focus, increase concentration, and offset mental fatigue. Rosemary increases memory retention and can act as a small pick-me-up on a morning when you're feeling physically or mentally exhausted. Rosemary and lemon in the morning combined with lavender and orange at night showed "significant improvement in personal orientation related to cognitive function" in patients with Alzheimer's disease with no noted side-effects (Buckle, 2014). The list goes on.

Now, there certainly could be placebo effects going on here, and that's where the research gets a bit fuzzy. For example, does peppermint increase alertness because of its inherent properties or because you are constantly spiking your coffee with peppermint creamer and have begun to associate staying awake with that smell? I've yet to find an answer.

Placebo or not, it may be worth piping some smells into your office during the workday. Or at least when you start to feel groggy and unfocused. Diffusers can be bought for less than $20 online. Grab one and experiment with different smells throughout the day. If you can find a scent that helps you focus on your most important work, you could regain $20 in lost time within a day.

The Sound of Productivity

If music can inspire, bring fear, or elicit tears of sadness and joy, could it also prime you for peak productivity and focus? It stands to reason that it should. After all, many people describe themselves as "fired up" or "in the zone" when listening to their favorite tunes. Queuing up Forgot About Dre while I'm working out is the equivalent of removing 50 pounds from my squat bar—I get pumped, and magically stronger. Or maybe it's that I'm more motivated.

My anecdotal 90s-hip-hop-evidence aside, research does suggest that music has a profound impact on mood. Further studies have connected this research to the art of getting things done. All told, when it comes to the question of whether music makes you more productive, the answer is absolutely, and it depends.

It depends on whether you are performing a rote task or are in deep thought. It depends on what scale the music is in. It depends on the volume of the music, the lyrics (if any), and the rhythm.

For boring, mindless, repetitive, or mundane tasks, upbeat, lyrical music in the major mode can improve happiness and mood, which leads to improved output. Next time you need to crush it while shoveling a driveway, performing data-entry, or cleaning house, choose songs like:

1. Brown Eyed Girl by Van Morrison

2. Rolling Stone by Bob Dylan

3. Let it Be by the Beatles

4. Ode to Joy by Beethoven

If, on the other hand, you're trying to learn, study, create, or think, that kind of music is a huge no-no. Despite mood improvements, the mental drain of high-energy, lyrical music is far too taxing, making it difficult to think deep thoughts, learn and recall new information, or remember complex tasks. If you're reading a book, thinking through a complicated problem, or writing a detailed Instagram post, avoid major mode music and instead choose something like:

1. Baroque classical

2. Ambient electronic

3. Video game music

This type of music blends into the background, is mellow and unobtrusive, doesn't have distracting high-high or low-low notes, lacks bothersome lyrics, and allows you to focus on the task at hand.

If you really want to focus, try listening to your music on repeat. Some people (including me) contend that listening to a song over and over helps them focus. I've noticed that it keeps my mind from wandering. After the second or third playback of the same song, it fades into the background while simultaneously blocking out true background noise.

If you usually work in silence, use these guidelines to put on some tunes and see if it positively affects your productivity. If you like listening to music while you work, use these guidelines to listen to the *right type* of music. Start building playlists of songs that work for you and make you more productive. In an age of limitless music through subscription services like Apple, Amazon, and Spotify, finding the right songs to help you focus, get creative, and get your most important work done is just a matter of effort.

The Sights of Productivity

Plants affect productivity. Smells affect productivity. Sounds and music affect productivity. And, colors do too.

In a study of participants taking an IQ test, those who took the test in rooms painted with cool colors (such as blue, grey, or white) performed better and showed a higher score than those in rooms with warmer, more stimulating colors (Belluck, 2009). That doesn't mean warm colors are bad. It means that brighter, warmer colors on the walls (like reds and oranges) should be reserved for creative work while cool colors are best for knowledge work or jobs that require concentration.

Whatever you do, make your environment as attractive and inviting as possible. Studies show that students, employees, and teams in manufacturing factories are more productive in attractive environments. Dull, cost-efficient, grey interiors with harsh lighting and industrial carpet (which describes every work environment created between 1960 and 2000) don't encourage or allow for maximum effectiveness at work (Hulshof, 2013).

Chapter Nineteen

Bringing It All Together

"You were born to win, but to be a winner, you must plan to win, prepare to win, and expect to win."

– Zig Ziglar

I know this Part V gave you a TON to consider. But I also worry that it might have overwhelmed to you. The good news is, even with full chapters on creating new expectations, keeping a productive mind, maintaining a productive body, and building a productive environment, we can boil everything down to a few simple reminders and habits.

So, let's recap what we learned and throw in a few extra tips for good measure. Choose just one to build into your habit routine (so as not to overwhelm yourself), and start tracking as your productivity grows:

- **Stop drinking caffeine 10 to 12 hours before bed.** Caffeine has a half-life of five to six hours, so drinking it too late leaves too much in your system when it's time for bed preventing adenosine from attaching to receptors in your brain to make you feel tired. This will either keep you awake or reduce the quality of your sleep, either of which hold drastic consequences for your ability to get things done.

- **Create a bedtime ritual.** Like a basketball player who performs the same routine before every free-throw, a bedtime ritual helps gear you up for sleep. Reading fiction is a great place to start, and a great way to end the day. Non-fiction can work but can wake your brain by giving you more to think about.

- **Keep the same sleep schedule every day.** Even on weekends. Irregular sleep tinkers with your circadian rhythm, making it difficult to focus and leaving you feel groggy. Yes, you'll have to make sacrifices some weekends to maintain the same sleep schedule. If you must get to bed late after a night of debauchery, keep your same wake up time. Your body will thank you when it's tired and ready to go to bed at your normal sleeping time the day after. Your mind will thank you when it doesn't feel the terrible effects of screwing up your circadian rhythm.

- **Spend 10 to 20 minutes every day in quiet meditation.** It may increase focus, improve working memory, and help you get in touch with your inner self. Be a witness to how this quiet meditation affects your ability to focus, concentrate, and get your most important work done.

- **Perform 20 to 30 minutes of light exercise every day.** Do it in the morning to get an energy boost throughout the day. Do it again in the afternoon if you feel groggy and need a pick-me-up.

- **Eat healthy, nutritious food that will give you sustained energy throughout the day.** Avoid the crashes and cravings that come from unhealthy, high glucose foods such as candy.

- **Manage your physical and mental stress to the right level.** Not so little that you feel inactive or laid back, but not so much that you feel fatigued or overwhelmed.

- **Keep live plants in your workspace within view.** A small, inexpensive investment in a hard-to-kill plant could make a noticeable difference and is worth buying immediately.

- **And my favorite:** If you're feeling particularly distracted, give your brain a dopamine hit with a work session at a coffee shop to help increase focus and energy for a few hours.

Finally, depending on the type of work that you are doing, set your environment for maximum productivity. It's best to work in daylight, in an environment which isn't too warm (causing drowsiness) or too cold (causing you to focus on retaining heat). Second, find a space with the right colors and smells a space with the right colors for the type of job you're performing and follow these guidelines:

Working on Detailed, Menial, Rote, or Physical Tasks?

1. Listen to upbeat music in the c-major scale.

2. Dab some peppermint essential oil in your wrists or neck, like cologne or perfume.

3. Work in a room with warm, invigorating colors.

Working on tasks that require concentration, focus, deep-thinking?

1. Listen to mellow and unobtrusive music without lyrics like Baroque Classical or Ambient Electronic.

2. Sip coffee before you get tired, allowing you to extend your working hours.

3. Diffuse rosemary or peppermint essential oil extract in your room.

4. Work in a room with dull, cool colors and lighting.

"A fundamental part of conscious evolution is learning to control and direct your attention — so that you can shine that spotlight onto what you want, rather than what you've been conditioned to want."

— Benjamin Hardy

Download the Mind, body, spirit checklist from www.michaelmehlberg.com/homeearly.

Part VI

Learning from Living

Bringing it all together for a productive, balanced life.

"It is not that we have a short time to live, but that we waste a lot of it. Life is long enough, and a sufficiently generous amount has been given to us for the highest achievements if it were all well invested. But when it is wasted in heedless luxury and spent on no good activity, we are forced at last by death's final constraint to realize that it has passed away before we knew it was passing. So it is: we are not given a short life but we make it short, and we are not ill-supplied but wasteful of it... Life is long if you know how to use it." — Seneca

^ Translation: Use what you've learned here to spend your life in a meaningful way.

Chapter Twenty

The Retrospective

"It is necessary to monitor your behavior if you wish to change it. Awareness is essential."

— Akiroq Brost

Once a month, our engineering team would get together to hold what we called a retrospective. At its core, this was a meeting to discuss three things:

1. What went well?
2. What needed to improve?
3. What would we commit to doing next?

Though only four weeks had passed between retrospectives, we'd accumulated enough lessons to identify plenty of areas to improve. Asking what went well ensured the team continued to focus on tasks and people and systems that had a positive influence on the outcome of our project. Asking what needed to improve was a constructive way of looking at our challenges and problems. Asking what we would commit to doing next focused us on the biggest problems—problems we would spend time and energy fixing in the following month.

To keep the productivity system you've built herein running smoothly and efficiently, we need to hold our own retrospective. Time spent thinking about what's working, what isn't, and what needs to happen next will pay off dividends.

"Knowing and understanding which decisions brought you to where you are now will help you to make better decisions in the future."

— Akiroq Brost

Now, because we don't learn as much in a week as we do in a month, and we don't learn as much in a month as we do in a year, I'm recommending multiple retrospectives to keep us on track. The first is a five-minute weekly retrospective. The second is slightly longer, but still brief monthly retrospective. And the final is a yearly retrospective where we pull out all the stops and really challenge ourselves to grow in the coming year.

The Weekly Retrospective

At the end of each week, spend five minutes (max) answering the following questions.

1. What should I double-down on?
2. What should I remove?
3. What needs to happen next week to keep me on track for the month?

1. What should I double down on?

Every day, dozens of shiny new ideas will present themselves to you, tugging at your attention, giving you an endless number of possible paths to follow. It's hard to ignore something that has the possibility of changing your life and work, and the fear of missing out

(FOMO) pushes us to take on more than we can afford. But the trouble with new ideas is they often seem more promising than they are.

Even *considering* a new ideas worth takes time. Not to mention, considering new ideas is a fantastic way to procrastinate real work.

So, if you must consider a new idea, consider it against the backdrop of what is already going well for you. Often, doubling down on what's working is a surer and safer way to getting better results faster. Considering a new idea against your already successful endeavors will temper your desire to take on the latest and greatest idea that's crossed your path.

When you double down on what is going well, you compound your results. You build momentum faster. Momentum that will carry you to your goals quicker than you thought possible. Doubling down on what is working well is how people achieve their goals early, or how they catch up after falling too far behind.

The thing you are doubling down on doesn't have to be grandiose. It could be incremental, minuscule, positive progress. The Japanese word Kaizen stands for continual, incremental self-improvement. It's a concept focused on getting 1% better every day. While 1% doesn't sound like much, it amounts to tremendous results. If you saved 1% more money every day, you'd *double* your money every 72 days. Focusing on improving those things that are going well in your system will compound into the same effect.

At your next retrospective, evaluate whether the time you've put into an activity is paying off in dividends or is just causing more work for not a lot of gain. If it's not paying off, consider removing it. If it is, double-down on it.

2. What should I remove?

Years ago, we took a family vacation to my parents' lake-cottage in Michigan. I had fond memories of fishing with my father and wanted to relive the experience with my own boys.

One early morning, we awoke, drove over to a small inland lake, and rented a rowboat. It took me five minutes to paddle out to our spot where we dropped anchor. It took only another five minutes for the complaining to start. My nine-year-old boy claimed he was getting seasick. My six-year-old boy said he was "soooo bored." Knowing their complaints would only get worse, I decided it best to row back to shore and find a different activity, like sleeping on the beach.

I started rowing but felt the wind at my back and couldn't seem to move anywhere. I rowed harder, but still barely moved toward shore. I became convinced that the blowing wind was pushing us back and preventing us from moving. Afraid that I'd be stuck in a rowboat with two hungry, bored children, I rowed with all my might. I rowed for 20 minutes straight. I rowed until my muscles gave out. And, when I finally looked up, frustration and sweat dripping from my brow, I found that we had barely moved at all. Worse, we were drifting right back to where we dropped anchor. At that moment, I was convinced we were stuck in some Bermuda-Triangle-like-lake-vortex, trapped for all time.

Just then, a small motorboat with two gents trolled over and asked if we needed a tug. With no energy or pride remaining, I agreed. They pulled us to shore, and as they motored away, I heard one man laughing hysterically while the other stood up to yell, "Hey buddy, your anchor was down!"

What little pride I'd regained during our ride sunk to the bottom of the lake where it still lies to this day. I had exhausted my mind and body rowing to shore only to get nowhere, all because my anchor was down. Now, safely docked, I pulled up my anchor to find it wrapped in 75 pounds of mud and seaweed that were dragging me down.

That's the thing about anchors. They don't just weigh you down, they get stuck in the mud. They get tangled in seaweed. They dig into the muck and kill all your momentum or prevent you from gaining any in the first place. Like my rowing efforts, if you don't take time to remove the anchors in your life, you'll expend a ton of energy without getting very far.

It sounds simple, yet, even knowing this, we all get as myopically focused on our goal as I did on the shore. We start hustling and grinding to get places without stopping to think. We ignore the anchors in life that drag us down and prevent us from making progress.

Each anchor may be small. Some anchors may seem like they'd take more effort and time to pull in than if we just kept rowing. But that's shortsighted. Life is a long game. There's no sprinting to the end.

Back to the question at hand, while my development team would ask, "what should we improve," I suggest asking, "what should I remove?" Some activities, tools, even people in your life don't support your goals. They are anchors that drag you down. These things don't need to be improved; they need to be cut from your life as quickly as possible. In a team setting, you're only as strong as your weakest link. For your own personal productivity, spending time trying to make a weak link stronger is wasteful. Instead, cut it, delegate it or ignore it all together.

Some anchors are internal in nature—excuses or fear, for example. Other anchors are external—distractions like television, social media, and video games. Belongings that you've gathered over the years or tools that no longer work. Even digital anchors like computer or phone apps that used to play a role in your life but now just clutter up your digital environment.

But the biggest anchors of all, the one that creates the most resistance, are toxic people. They can be negative, pessimistic, and unsupportive. Pull those anchors up one by one, thank them for their role in your life, and leave them behind. Replace them with people who care about you, wo care about what you're doing, and who are supportive of your goal. Doing so is the equivalent of adding another rower to your boat.

What or who is dragging you down? What are those things that hold you back? Who are those people that are resisting your growth or planting seeds of failure in your mind?

3. What needs to happen next week to keep me on track for the month?

Every week, after answering the previous two questions, prioritize the list of things you'd love to double-down on and a list of anchors holding you back. Identify the most important changes, tasks, or projects you can complete in the next week that will help you take the biggest step toward to your monthly goals.

Since you've already listed the work that you want to double-down on, selecting one of those to focus on in the coming week should be simple. Since you've already identified your anchors, selecting one you want to cut in the upcoming week should be easy. And, since you've already broken down your monthly goals into weekly goals in Chapter Eight, selecting what to work on in the upcoming week should be cake.

We all have the same 24 hours in a day. It's the people that decide what to double-down on, what to remove, and what's most important to work on next that make the most progress.

#

This retrospective process shouldn't take longer than 20 minutes. Five minutes thinking about what you need to double down on, another five thinking about what anchors are holding you back, then five more planning out what you'll work on in the coming weeks is all you need. Fifteen minutes getting clear on what needs to be done leaves five minutes for scheduling these priorities as tasks you'll get to work on in the coming week.

Like I mentioned in the beginning of this chapter, we need to keep our system in good working order. Asking these questions are the equivalent of oiling up your productivity machine.

Stopping to reflect on what's helping you make progress and what's holding you back is a helpful way to call a time-out, gather your wits, and decide what's the next most important thing to get done. Acting on what you discover from this retrospective will help you make incremental, continual progress that will compound in the weeks, months, and years to come.

The Monthly Retrospective

The end of every month is a time for reflection. Deeper than the end of every week, but not as much as at the end of every year.

In any given month, you can accomplish quite a lot. You might finish a project. You might start a new one. You might have established new habits and learned new skills that are paying off (or are wasting your time). Now, at the end of every month, is the time to reflect on what's working, what isn't, and what you can do in the next month to further refine your system.

Since we're digging a bit deeper than we do in the weekly retrospective, we'll want to spend more time reflecting, but no more than 30 minutes. We'll also want to ask slightly different questions.

Questions aimed at taking a broader look at what's happening in your work and life and what needs to be done for the remainder of the year. At the end of every month, ask yourself:

1. What successes have I had that I can build on?
2. What am I wasting time on?
3. What can I do in the next 30 days that will make for an awesome month no matter what else happens?

1. What successes have I had that I can build on?

In 2006, our small business was awarded a large and super geeky government research grant to study cyber security in software systems. We were thrilled beyond believe. Not only because we'd have more cash in our coffers than Walter White in Breaking Bad, but because it guaranteed our team work for the next 24 months. Believe me, in a small business when you're working paycheck to paycheck, two years of certainty is wildly exciting.

But our initial excitement soon wore off and we were hit with the doldrums of detailed technical work. Days turned to weeks; weeks crawled into months. At the end of the first year, we were battle-hardened researchers, no longer interested in the results and no longer excited by the work. That is, until we all realized how our small, excited team had turned into a trudging group of busy bees'.

We decided it was time to celebrate. Nothing big. Nothing extravagant. Just a team picnic at the local park to reward ourselves for a year of hard work and lighten the load for the year to come. The celebration, though small, was so refreshing we found ways of celebrating small again in the near future. Before too long, we had made it a point to celebrate every small milestone, building our confidence and excitement of coming into work each day for the remainder of the second year.

If you go too long without reminding yourself of how far you've come, you'll just end up goal-chasing like we did. Accomplishment turns into a slog as you move from one achievement to the next without taking the time to appreciate what you've done. So, once a month, as part of your monthly retrospective, ask yourself what successes you've had. What are your winning achievements? What are the things that have made you the proudest? Then, celebrate them!

After you've taken yourself out to dinner or bought yourself a fun, small, geeky gadget to reward yourself for a job well done, ask yourself, of all these successes, where do I have the most momentum? What's hot right now? What's really going well? Where do you feel the most confident? What can you build on in the coming month to keep the momentum and excitement flowing?

Then, just like the weekly retrospective, double-down on those areas that are going well and bringing you more reasons to celebrate for achieving your goals.

2. What am I wasting time on?

For everything that's gone well in the past month, there are likely areas that need improvement. Neglecting those areas will fester from a small itch into a sore that will prevent you from running full speed ahead.

As I already mentioned, I once got on the meditation bandwagon. I had tried meditation in high school, then again in college. I heard about the benefits of meditation from Tim Ferriss and other life coaches who promoted the amazing positive effects on their blogs and podcasts. From time to time, I would read about meditation in some Zen or martial arts book and give it another go. When popular media started talking about it, I gave it a serious go and integrated it into my system.

Every morning, I'd wake up 30 minutes early. After spending nine minutes putting on pants, stumbling downstairs, and starting the coffee, I'd set a time for 21 minutes and meditate. For months this went on. Some mornings I'd get the effects I was looking for, other mornings I wouldn't. But because it was in my system, I never missed a day. Until I performed a retrospective like the one we're outlining in this chapter.

After a few months of trying, became clear to me that, even if there were benefits to meditation, I wasn't feeling them. It wasn't clarifying my thinking. It wasn't giving me superpowers. It wasn't helping me focus or relax or connect with my work in any ways the experts claimed.

I took a hard look at whether this meditation cog in my machine was helping the other cogs turn. Ultimately, I decided that, while there may be unseen benefits, it wasn't right for my system. So, I thought about where those extra 30 minutes should be going and ultimately replaced meditation with journaling.

Come next month's retrospective, I could feel the difference. Journaling was giving me huge benefits. It helped me focus on my work. With a cup of coffee and a burning candle, I could use my journal to reflect on my progress. I could pep-talk myself into a plan for the day.

More so, it was the most blissful time of my day, set me in the right mood, started me down the right path, and granted me far more insight than meditation ever had. Replacing the meditation cog with a journaling cog had my machine oiled, dust-free, and running like a champion.

In case it's not clear, I'm not saying you shouldn't try meditation, or that you should drop it if you are already doing so. I sometimes still feel inclined to meditate. What I am saying is that, through this monthly retrospective process, I found a part of my system that was taking time with no meaningful return; time that could have been focused on something else. Removing that wasted time granted me the mental energy to do something that mattered more.

You need to find what works for you. And you can't do that by trying the same tired things over and over, hoping they change and give you a positive effect. Once you identify time wasters like mine, you can focus yourself on where to improve. Perhaps you've fallen behind on learning about a new skill that will help you achieve your goals. Or maybe you've gone slack on your daily planning and scheduling. Whatever it is, pointing out to yourself where those problems are, why they are problematic, and fixing them in the coming month will keep you running fast and smooth.

Finally, you don't have to improve at everything, nor does everything you waste time on have to be dropped completely. Ask yourself what you are continuing to do yourself that you are not good at. Maybe horsing around with your website is both a way for you to procrastinate and is turning your website into a hot mess. Turn it over to a web developer, someone who is trained and skilled at doing this job. Whatever it is, you have only three options when you find that you're not good at doing something yourself but need to get it done.

1. Get better at it
2. Delegate it
3. Kill it

3. What can I do in the next 30 days that will make for an awesome month, no matter what else happens?

Finally, if you're like me, your to-do list reaches from here to the moon. You have big goals to achieve, and a dozen or more skills you wish to learn.

I struggle with keeping focused on skills that matter to my goals. I'm interested in learning chess, guitar, video games, science, and technology. I love reading about new discoveries and reading biographies of legendary people like Leonardo da Vinci, Thomas Edison, and Steve Jobs. All of these activities are great, but I have to take care to not let them leech over into the time I have to work on what matters.

We can temper these interests by looking ahead and narrowing our focus. Not to two or three things, but to one thing that matters most. Looking ahead to the next month, what is that one thing that really gets your blood pumping? Something that, even if it were the only thing you finished, would excite you, make you feel a sense of accomplishment, and accelerate your progress toward your goals for the year. Once you've identified that thing, you can ask yourself what little leaps you can make to get there.

The Yearly Retrospective

"At the end of each December, I spend time reflecting on the past year. First, I take my calendar for the year and review how I spent my time. I think and process and pray about the year. Then I capture some thoughts on paper."

— John C. Maxwell, Thinking for a Change

The new year always starts off with a bang. We have our New Year's resolutions, fresh goals in mind, and a direction in which to sail. After a few months, we're in the thick of things. Then, at the end of the year comes this big crescendo where work releases us to our friends and families, and we go crazy buying gifts for everyone we know. Once all of that is over though, I come down off my holiday high and feel a natural sense of introspection before the next year starts.

Many years ago, I read John C. Maxwell's "Thinking for a Change", a fantastic book about being thoughtful, using your mind, planning, and better thinking. Some of his questions—questions he would ask himself to reflect on his accomplishments and build a plan for his future—were questions I captured in my journal. I'd discover more great books such as "The ONE Thing" by Gary Keller and thoughtful podcasts such as "The Tim Ferriss Show," adopting select insights into the following list of year reflections.

1. What have I accomplished this past year?

2. What were my big business highlights?

3. What were my big personal highlights?

4. What were my low points?

5. Do I have any reflections of significance?

6. Where am I in my journey?

7. What is my zenith?

8. What is my new story?

By taking the time to ask these questions of ourselves at the end of each year, we can wrap our head around what will be important in the year to come.

What have I accomplished this past year?

Look over your goals and review the progress you've made. Look at each area of your life and think about where you've come in the past year and what achievements you've made. For business, what were your big business highlights? What about your personal highlights? List them all and be specific. Talk about how those accomplishments made you feel. List any major events that happened. And, when you're done there, list any other reflections of significance.

Don't think too much about these. If it comes to mind, jot it down. And don't think you have to spend oodles of time capturing *every* accomplishment. What's important is to reflect on your year, recognize those accomplishments that come to mind, and write them down. By capturing them for future reference, you'll realize how much you've grown. And, that's something to be proud of.

> "At the end of each December, I spend time reflecting on the past year. First, I take my calendar for the year and review how I spent my time. I think and process and pray about the year. Then I capture some thoughts on paper."
>
> — John C. Maxwell, Thinking for a Change

Business Highlights

1. _____

2. _____

3. _____

#1 Business Highlight?

_____

_____

_____

Personal Highlights

1. _____

2. _____

3. _____

#1 Personal Highlights?

_____

_____

_____

Major Events

  1. _____

  2. _____

  3. _____

  4. _____

  5. _____

Personal Reflections of Significance

_____

_____

_____

What were my low points?

No year is completely filled with growth and accomplishment. There are always low points. Maybe you didn't get that promotion you felt you deserved. Maybe you had a goal to start a business and never got around to it. Maybe you lost a job you love because of a global pandemic.

Write these low points down. Acknowledge their existence. Gain perspective on and power over them. Think about whether that low point mattered to you, whether you want to adjust and fix it in the coming year, or if it just doesn't matter.

Assuming you aren't happy with these low points, ask yourself, how do I remove them from my life? Where can you place your focus to ensure these low points, or others like them, don't happen again in the future?

_____

_____

_____

Where am I in my journey?

We're all on a journey to somewhere. Many people don't know where they're going. Nor do they know where they are. The goal of this question is to identify both.

What's going on right now with your career, your business, your family, your friends? Where are you, currently, for each important area of your life. Don't think about it too much, just write down what you feel.

Also, write down what you are particularly good at. You're probably better now at different things than you were a year prior, and that's part of your journey. Capture them so you can later identify how to get great at them.

_____

_____

_____

What is my (new) zenith?

I know, I know, we've already spent scads of time identifying our purpose in Part II. But it's worth reviewing every year. Because a year is a long time, and people change. When you change, you learn a bit more about yourself and may have further insight or modifications to your purpose that you didn't realize before.

Review your current zenith. Then, take a few moments to identify any refinements you can make to it for the coming year.

_____

_____

_____

What is my new story?

The story we tell ourselves about our life, our achievements, and what we believe we can achieve bound our upper limits. Expanding this upper limit allows us to continually learn, accomplish new things, and realize our goals, vision, and purpose.

You previously wrote down what you were good at. Now ask yourself what you can become great at. What changes would you make right now, immediately, if money weren't an issue, if you followed your gut, and didn't care what anyone else thought? What are some things you can no longer accept in your life? What are new things you must have in your life? What's holding you back? What people should you be surrounding yourself with in your new self? Who do you need to cut out? These questions will help you craft new expectations and a new story for yourself that you can work on in the coming years.

But to really put a point on it, do one simple exercise. If you're using pen and paper, draw a line down the middle of your page. On the left, write your current story, the one you captured in this very section. On the right, write your new story, the one you're capturing now with the questions we just went over.

Now look at the transformation that needs to happen between the two sides and think about what goals you should have, what you have to do, and what you have to avoid to make that transformation happen in the coming year.

_____

_____

_____

_____

_____

_____

Chapter Twenty-One

Checks and Balances

"He who learns but does not think, is lost! He who thinks but does not learn is in great danger."

— Confucius

It's a well-known fact of thermodynamics that every closed system tends toward chaos. Take my house, for example. If left alone while the kids are home, it begins to look messy after 15 minutes. After an hour, it turns into a fucking landfill.

Our lives aren't closed systems, but this productivity system we've created here is. Our purpose and vision and goals are defined, our habits are set, and if we don't keep our system in good working order, it will tend back to the chaos we previously faced (and found overwhelming).

As an example, if you create a new habit that isn't doing its job, you now have one more thing to do but won't have anything to show for it (besides lost time and energy). If you complete a goal early but don't set a new one, the extra time you would have spent working toward that new goal will be spent on frivolous activities that don't help you realize your vision.

When you think of building a system, it's easy to imagine a machine full of gears all working together. One gear is your purpose. One is your vision. A few other gears are your goals. A bunch of other smaller gears are the tips and tactics to protect your time, maximize your output, and get the most out of your day. Turn one gear, and the entire machine turns; your entire purpose moves forward.

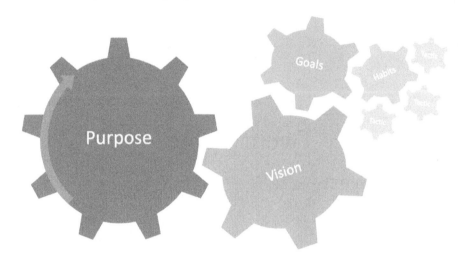

But life isn't a machine. Life isn't a series of gears that all work in lockstep to tick you closer and closer to your true self. Life is messy, disorganized, and almost everything is out of your control. As such, the machine you've created throughout this book won't stay in pristine working order without your diligence. Setbacks will cause it to rust. Unanticipated issues will fill it with dirt and grime. Without proper care, the system we've created here will gum itself up with the stickiness of life.

Unfortunately, you can't deal with these issues by taking one gear out and replacing it with a fresh one. That's the life-hack approach. That's the thinking that leads to frustration; when you mistakenly believe that one shiny new gear (a hack) will make the entire machine work wonders. In reality, a new shiny gear turns the machine the same speed as an older gear of the same size. And, regardless of how new that gear is, it can't turn a machine caked in dirt and rust.

We also can't crank the gears harder. We can't make the machine run faster than it should for a long period of time. That's the "push, push, push" version of productivity; when you believe that working longer and harder is the answer to getting more done. It works for a while, but soon enough the gears wear out and the machine grinds to a halt.

That's why it's critical to inspect this machine regularly. We have to look at each gear and assess whether it's performing optimally. We have to look at this machine overall to see whether it's moving us toward our goals. We have to oil the squeaky gears, blow dust out of the dirty ones, and pull out the cruft that gets caught up in them over time.

Regular maintenance is necessary for this system. Instead of waiting until the system no longer works, your goals are too far off to manage, your habits have atrophied, and your skills haven't grown, we need to check in regularly to assess where we are vs. where we want to be. After all, it's easier to fix a machine that has some dirt slowing things down than it is to wait until that same machine is rusted out, crammed with debris, and no longer working.

Adjusting Course

Our company CEO sat across from me with a seriousness about him that I knew meant business. I was leading our software engineering team toward a September delivery date for a high-profile customer, and we were a month behind schedule.

Moments after I'd emailed our CEO to tell him we would deliver late, he was sitting across from me, pointing out in no uncertain terms that we would *not* miss that date. The goal wasn't changing. Nor was it moving. So, I needed to play the game differently.

Like my project, most goal's never track perfectly to completion. They are messy, living beasts affected by outside events and unforeseen factors. But, while there's no use fighting it, we also can't simply let our goals slip without adjusting course. If things get really out of whack, if one of your goals get so far off there's no hope of accomplishing it, you can do one of two things:

1. Leave the goal the same but change the way you work toward it such that you have a higher likelihood of hitting it.

2. Change the goal.

Of course, moving the goalpost would be a third option. But I don't recommend it. Moving the goalpost sends the wrong message to yourself; that you don't take your goals seriously. It sends a message that, if the mountain you're climbing gets to tough, you can just chop off the peak and claim victory when you reach the (flattened, lower) top. If you move the goalpost, you're telling yourself that success is more important than integrity. You're saying that success can be bought, not earned. All of this is destructive—a mindset that will erode your inner confidence and make it more difficult to set and achieve challenging goals in the future.

This is why my CEO wasn't letting me off the hook. He wouldn't allow me to move the goalpost. And, since the customer had already paid us for our delivery, we couldn't change the goal. So, with no relief coming, we regrouped as a team, made some smart and drastic changes in the way we worked to achieve our goal, and ended up finishing on time and on budget.

The fact of the matter is, nobody cares about your goals more than you. So, you need to care about them and respect them enough to maintain them, work toward them, and strive for them through good times and bad.

If and when you get behind, recalculate what you need to do to meet your goal. Figure out a different plan of attack to get there. If meeting that goal is truly impossible, keep pushing hard to the end. You won't know if the goal is complete or not until you reach the finish line. When you do, and if your goal isn't met, don't beat yourself up. Just mark that goal as failed. Then learn from it. Realize that, though you didn't hit your target, you still made progress. Reflect on why it failed and create a new goal that's specific, measurable, achievable, relevant, and time bound. Break that new goal down. Track its progress daily. Create lead measures that are fully in your control and will help you take the necessary action to make your goal a reality. Success will come.

One Final Check (and Balance)

I'm not a financial advisor, and I don't play one on TV. But I know that, when it comes to investing, you want a balanced portfolio. This means spreading your money around; keeping some of your assets in cash, others in bonds, and others in stocks.

For example, you don't want to store your entire life's savings in heater vent in your baby's room, Breaking Bad Style. If your house burns down, you are s.c.r.e.w.e.d. If you forget where it is, you'll drive yourself into a panic-induced anxiety coma looking for it. If your baby grows up, finds it, and loses it all playing Blackjack at a local casino, there ain't no getting it back.

On the flip side, you don't want to keep your entire portfolio in the stock market. Stocks can be volatile, and if the market drops its pants like it did during the Great Depression, or in 1937, or in 1962, or in 2008, or during the great covid-19 panic of 2020, it drops out for you too. You lose a significant portion of your investments and can't retire until you're dead.

A balanced portfolio is one that has some assets in cash, some assets in bonds, some assets in mutual funds, some assets in stocks, etc. Not equal amounts of money. Equal amounts of risk vs. reward. If done properly, the likelihood that any one asset class loses value is 100%, but the likelihood that *every* asset class drops is highly improbable. As such, you minimize your risk of losing everything.

Now, over time, you'll do better with some investments than others. Your nice balanced portfolio will start to get unbalanced. Whereas you may have started with 25% of your assets in cash, 15% in stocks, 20% in bonds, and 40% in mutual funds, these percentages will change as the markets grow and shrink. Your stocks may start doing extremely well in a bull year, making them worth 40% of your total portfolio. Congrats! You've made some money. But now you're out of balance. You now have too much risk in stock, and it's a good idea to reinvest that additional 25% into your bonds, cash, and mutual funds. In other words, it's a good idea to bring all of your investments back into their original balance. That's what it means to rebalance your portfolio, and you should do it with your time too.

Remember your time pie from Chapter Three? Each slice represented a different aspect of your day. You decided how big your sleep piece, your exercise piece, your marketing, planning, relaxing, and all other pieces should be. Like your investment portfolio though, your priorities will force your ideal time pie out of balance.

You'll know it's happening when you're checking emails during dinner or when you're marketing your business all day without working on important projects. Or when you realize that it's October and you hadn't read a single book all year (personal story from a few years ago). Or, maybe you have to take a late-night flight to a meeting and lose a bit of sleep. Then the next day you stay out late with a client and lose some more. Then a late-night flight home. You get back to the office and find that everyone needs your time, you have 9000 emails to catch up on, and the project that was doing well before you left is falling apart. Another late night for you, and lost sleep. After a week of this, you notice that the eight hours of sleep that you need to be consistently productive is no longer. You're only getting six. Time to rebalance.

Granted, not every day is going to fit perfectly into your plan. It doesn't work that way for finance, and it won't work that way for your time. There are simply too many variables, too many interruptions that can get you off balance on any given day. But, on the whole, check to ensure your time portfolio is balanced the way you like it. And, just like in finance, if any one activity or asset gets too big (or small), take from one and give to something else until balance is restored.

"Better things than fighting, should a Jedi Master be doing! Seeking wisdom. Finding balance."

—Yoda

Chapter Twenty-Two

Everything Works Together

"The more moving parts you have, the greater the chance you have
for a breakdown."

— Coach Denny Crum

During one family vacation, I stepped in a hole while playing tag with my kids on the beach. If there's a sure way to twist a knee, it's sticking your foot in the sand and turning your body hard. The damage wasn't permanent, but it took a few weeks to heal.

A full year later, on the heels of back to back business travel, this once-healed knee injury flared up again. I wasn't hobbling around, but it bothered me.

I tried Advil. I tried ice. I even tried walking differently. No single thing I did seemed to shake it. This went on for months until I spoke to my personal trainer.

"Bruh, you're old as shit. You've got to take care of your joints." (Yes, this is how he talks to me). Satisfied that I had been verbally abused enough, he diagnosed the problem and suggested a few things:

217

stop stressing my joints by crossing my legs when I sit, stop pounding my joints by replacing dress shoes with tennis shoes while traveling, and stop putting pressure on my joints by checking my bags instead of carrying them with me through airports.

I *had* considered these to be stressors on my knee but hadn't considered stopping them all at once. Many people wore dress shoes through the airport, how much damage could that really do? I liked my duffel bag and backpack, and I didn't like my roller bag. Surely carrying 20 pounds of clothing wasn't hurting things. Crossing my legs was comfortable and natural. How much could that really hurt?

The thing was, none of these individual stressors was the cause of my pain. It was all of them together. Walking through the airport in dress shoes while carrying 20 pounds of luggage before sitting at the gate with my legs crossed combined to prevent my knee from healing. Any single change would make only a slight difference. But all changes together would rid me of this pain entirely. I was fully healed in two weeks.

I realized, after the fact, that I wasn't considering the whole system. I wasn't considering where different stresses were coming from that kept my knee from healing. And I wasn't able to actually heal my knee until I took all those stressors into account.

Great story, Mike, but what the fuck are you trying to tell me? Good question. I'm trying to tell you this…

It's easy to get the big things right, but it's the little things that matter

Right now, you may be thinking of taking some pieces of this system to use and leaving the rest behind. Some of my ideas seem whacked out, odd, inconsequential, or even unimportant. But to ignore them is the productivity equivalent of continuing to walk through the airport with dress shoes on, carrying a heavy load on an already-injured knee.

Lose focus on your purpose and you'll be a rudderless ship, drifting in the wind. You won't have a guiding light to tell you what productive work is and isn't. And, since you won't know what matters, anything and everything becomes a distraction. You'll find yourself wasting time on unimportant things like social media, television, and news. You'll find yourself searching your inbox for something to do.

Muddy your vision and you'll lose sight of how you want your days to look. You'll miss those activities that give you energy and make your time feel well spent. The broken days will add up to broken weeks, leading to broken months and broken years that don't look or feel anything like the one you designed.

Lose sight of your goals and you'll be back to not getting anything done. You'll be working towards an unknown, distracted by other people's problems, wondering how you are ever going to get ahead. Without goals to drive you toward your vision and purpose, your chances of making either of them a reality are nearly zero. Goals take luck out of the equation. Lose sight of them, and luck is all you'll have to rely on.

See where I'm going with this? Good, but I'm not done.

Stray from tracking and developing your habits and skills and you'll find the path to your goals long and strenuous. It will be hard to gain momentum, never optimizing yourself for those things you could be doing efficiently, never learning the skills that will make the trek toward your goals faster and easier.

Miss your daily, weekly, monthly, or yearly planning and you'll be back to fighting against your will. Instead of doing what you've planned and scheduled you'll be constantly deciding whether to procrastinate or work, rest or push forward, focus on task A or task B. Before the end of the day, decision fatigue will set in and you'll go right back to your old ways. Ways that keep you late in the office and unbalanced in life.

Skip those retrospective exercises and you'll never learn. You'll never be able to see the forest for the trees, always wondering why that new tactic you are experimenting with isn't working out and never knowing how much time and energy it's really costing you to keep using it.

Even ignoring the tactics outlined in Part I like getting your environment in shape for maximum productivity, learning how to say "no," and listening to the right music during different kinds of work could have drastic consequences on how much or little you are able to accomplish on any given day. Miss out on an hour or two of sleep and you'll become irritable, unable to make clear decisions, and far less productive than normal. Eat crappy food for too long and your body won't have the energy it needs to get through the day. Think you don't have time for exercise, and you'll lose out on the energy benefits exercise gives you in the afternoon, right around that time when you'll start feeling a normal post-lunch lull.

The little things matter. Not each one individually. All of them. Together. All the little things all together make all the difference in the world. It's the difference between being a slightly more productive and having the time in your day to pursue your purpose and passion while still maintaining balance in life and at work.

One Final Little Thing That Matters

Vision, goals, and plans, by their very nature, force you to confront all that you want but don't have. They can sometimes leave you feeling negative.

Spend too long thinking about how to move from the life you're living to the vision you have and you'll start feeling like an underachiever. Stare for too long at how far away your goals are and you'll be in danger of beating yourself up for not being where you need to be. Follow and respect and admire your heroes, people who seem have everything you want, and you'll lose sight of what you already have—everything in your life to be thankful for.

Which brings me to my final thing that matters: gratitude.

Leave time every day for gratitude. Gratitude keeps you grounded. Gratitude maintains a winning mindset. Gratitude is the foundation of your character, the beginnings of new relationships, and the appreciation of existing ones. Furthermore, expressing your thanks can improve your overall well-being, increase happiness, even strengthen self-control ("Giving thanks," n.d.).

Personality and Individual Differences published a study in 2012 citing that grateful people feel healthier, have fewer aches and pains, exercise more often, and generally take better care of themselves (Morin, 2015). Oh, and remember how important sleep is from Chapter Sixteen? Yeah, according to Applied Psychology: Health and Well-being, gratitude helps you sleep better too (Digdon & Koble, 2011).

There are dozens of other scientifically proven benefits of gratitude that can be found with a quick Google search. I'll let you poke around for them yourself. In the meanwhile, keep striving for your vision and keep planning for your goals. But also take time to be grateful for what you already have. In a world of future visions and unrealized goals and unmet plans, gratitude is the antidote for want.

Fortunately, hundreds of gratitude practices already exist. Here are a few I've found helpful to staying grounded and focused on the positive, starting with my favorite:

1. Keep a gratitude journal. This can be a separate journal where you opine for 15 minutes on all the things you are thankful for, or a simple line in your daily planner to state one thing you are grateful for on this day. I personally write a single line in my daily planner. It takes less than 30 seconds, but causes me to remember that, for all the unmet goals in my life, I have many really great things going for me already that I shouldn't lose sight of.

2. Reach out to someone, thanking them for their role in your life. A phone call or hand-written, snail-mail letter if you have the time or feel so impassioned. Even a text message or email will do the trick. The second you send it, you'll feel good. Most of the time, those people will write you back. That's when you'll feel great.

3. Help someone do something. Anything. Help your spouse carry the groceries in. Help your kid with their homework. Help a random stranger by holding the door for them. These small gestures show others you are grateful for them, even if you don't know them. You'll get a little hit of dopamine, forget about all those stressors in your life, and immediately feel like a better human being.

4. Just reflect. You don't even have to do anything. You can just sit there like a bump on a pickle and quietly meditate on whatever comes to mind that you're grateful for. Before I made a more conscious practice of daily gratitude writing, I would wake up and spend the first 30 seconds next to my bed just

thinking about how lucky I am for all that I have. It was almost as good as a cup of coffee.

Take 30 seconds to be grateful for something, no matter how small, every day. And, if ever in doubt of what you should be grateful for, follow the advice of Ralph Waldo Emerson.

"Cultivate the habit of being grateful for every good thing that comes to you, and to give thanks continuously. And because all things have contributed to your advancement, you should include all things in your gratitude."

— Ralph Waldo Emerson

Chapter Twenty-Three

To the Moon!

> "Bit by bit, putting it together...
> Piece by piece, only way to make a work of art.
> Every moment makes a contribution,
> Every little detail plays a part.
> Having just the vision's no solution,
> Everything depends on execution,
> Putting it together, that's what counts."

— Stephen Sondheim, Sunday in the Park with George

In 1962, President John F. Kennedy toured the NASA Space Center on Merritt Island, Florida. As the story goes, the President took a wrong turn during his tour and paused to speak with an unassuming gentleman sweeping the floor in a service hallway.

"What do you do here?" the president asked.

The question seemed silly. Everyone knew the man was a janitor. But without missing a beat, the man responded, "Mr. President, I'm helping put a man on the moon."

223

This guy wasn't building rockets. He wasn't programming flight computers. He wasn't an astronaut in training, preparing his body and mind for the dangers of space travel. He was sweeping the floor. But he knew his purpose, better than most. And this purpose drove his every move.

From the first word of this book, we learned what productivity is and isn't. We learned that the old way of being productive—running around like headless chickens, working relentlessly on task after task until we flop into bed from exhaustion—isn't productive. We also learned that popular myths like working more hours to get more done, staying productive for hours and days at a time, or mimicking the routines of billionaires to be successful just aren't true. Waking up early to work more hours is hard without purpose. Doing what billionaires do won't make a difference because billionaires work on what matters to them and we need to work on what matters to us.

What is true is that clarity of purpose is the single biggest way to prevent distractions. With purpose, we can develop a vision and goals and habits and skills that take us from where we are to where we want to go.

I hope that this book has helped you find the purpose and clarity that this janitor has. Clarity to help you focus on what matters. Clarity that will help you get more out of life. Clarity that will allow you to crush your day, live in balance, and get home early to spend time on that which matters most to you.

You know now why purpose is that lighthouse guiding you through calm waters and treacherous storms. You now understand why having a vision is important to defining how you live as you sail daily toward your purpose. You know why goals are important to realizing your vision and purpose, and how to break those goals down into small milestones and trackable habits to help you build momentum in the year to come.

What's more, you know some of the science behind those productivity tactics that can help you get more done. You know how to integrate them into your day. And, you know how to deal with incoming requests and interruptions, protect your time by saying "no," avoid the fear of missing out, and manage that which is out of your control.

Finally, you know how to learn and adjust your system, doubling down on what's working and asking yourself the right questions to shed what isn't.

These things, all together, are what it takes to get home early. It's not complicated, but it's not easy either. You'll have to work at it. And, if you do, you'll find that feeling at the end of the day when you know you've crushed it; when you've accomplished everything you wanted to and more. You finish early, and be ready to head home to rest, relax, and recharge with friends and family, only to wake up with a plan you can use to crush tomorrow, and the day after, and the day after that.

That's the feeling we're going after, and the results. They won't come from doing one thing different. They come from applying the process, the systems, and the science outlined in this book to your life in a way that that aligns with your purpose, that fulfills your goals, and that makes sense to your life. And now you know how to do it.

#

This system will challenge your instincts, will test your discipline, and will, at first, seem to get in the way of "how things have always been done." It's those times when you're failing hard that you'll need to keep focused on the reason why you read this book in the first place. It's those times where you feel like you don't have time to plan your day, schedule your tasks, or perform that end-of-month retrospective that you'll need to remember why you started and what you hoped to get out of it.

"Winning is not at sometime thing it's an all the time thing. You don't win once in a while, you don't do things right once in a while. You do them right all the time. Winning is habit. Unfortunately, so is losing"

— Vince Lombardi

Because when you fail, and you will, it's how you respond that matters. When your friends and family and coworkers start questioning what you are doing, and they will, brush off the criticism. They haven't walked in your shoes. They don't know your potential. And, they haven't tried this system (give them this book, maybe they should).

They don't know the importance of purpose, vision, goals, habits, etc. in protecting your time so you can spend more time with them. They're being critical, and it's not the critic who counts…

"It is not the critic who counts; not the man who points out how the strong man stumbles, or where the doer of deeds could have done them better. The credit belongs to the man who is actually in the arena, whose face is marred by dust and sweat and blood; who strives valiantly; who errs, who comes short again and again, because there is no effort without error and shortcoming; but who does actually strive to do the deeds; who knows great enthusiasms, the great devotions; who spends himself in a worthy cause; who at the best knows in the end the triumph of high achievement, and who at the worst, if he fails, at least fails while daring greatly, so that his place shall never be with those cold and timid souls who neither know victory nor defeat."

— Theodore Roosevelt

#

As my lead technologist sat in front of me in her performance review, tears streaming down her face over her pending divorce, I wanted to give her her marriage back. I wanted to show her the science proving that her incredible results at work couldn't last if she lost the very thing that mattered most to her.

As I listened to my own son, struggling to get a handle on seemingly insurmountable choices, I wanted to snap my fingers and show him all the little things I'd learned to prioritize and focus on what matters; preventing his frustration and eliminating the discomfort from his day.

And as I listened to the chaos and disarray in the San Francisco loan officers life, living under constant pressure and hoping that the seconds saved by building a bathroom in his office would help him remove feelings of overwhelm, I wanted to share with him this very system for crushing his day job while still having the time and energy left at night for relationships, rest, and relaxation.

But I couldn't, because this book didn't exist yet.

Now it does. And now you've been exposed to a system and scientific research that has the potential to turn an otherwise chaotic, disorganized, stressful life into a structured, designed life where your ideas and thoughts turn into actions that make a positive difference and take you to where you always wanted to be.

We were never taught how to realize our vision. We were never taught how to set goals, break them down, and track them to achievement. We had to learn on our own.

But now, having learned how to do so, we no longer stand on the side of the river full of people full of doubt, unsure of how to cross the turbulent rapids to the other side. We now have the system and tools to stand on the other side of that river. The side that is full of happy, organized, productive people living the life they want. Not a lavish life. Not a life of excess. Just a mostly untroubled life of accomplishment and relative peace. A balanced life. A life where you can, more often than not, get home early.

References

Barlett, A. (2018, September 12). 3 Surprising Secrets to Maintaining Your Focus. Medium. Retrieved from https://medium.com/taking-note/3-surprising-secrets-to-maintaining-your-focus-49046af171ac

Become a Corporate Drone in 30 Days or Less: Step-By-Step Instructions on How to Stop Thinking for Yourself, Kiss Ass Like a Pro & Wear Black Like a Champ. (n.d.). Retrieved from http://accounts.themiddlefingerproject.org/become-a-corporate-drone-in-30-days-or-less-step-by-step-instructions-on-how-to-stop-thinking-for-yourself-kiss-ass-like-a-pro-wear-black-like-a-champ/

Belluck, P. (2009, February 6). Colors may affect performance, study suggests. The New York Times. Retrieved from https://www.nytimes.com/2009/02/06/health/06iht-color.1.19983382.html

Bradford & Desrochers. (2009). The use of scents to influence consumers: the sense of using scents to make cents. Journal of Business Ethics.

Bradshaw, A. (n.d.). The World's Most Productive Countries and How to Replicate at Work. Expert Market. Retrieved from https://www.expertmarket.co.uk/crm-systems/the-ultimate-guide-to-work-place-productivity

Britton, B. and Tesser, A. (1991, September). Effects of Time-Management Practices on College Grades. Journal of Educational Psychology.

Buckle, J. (2014, November 14). Clinical Aromatherapy - E-book: Essential Oils in Practice. Elsevier Health Sciences.

Clear, J. (n.d.) How Long Does it Actually Take to Form a New Habit? (Backed by Science). James Clear. Retrieved from https://jamesclear.com/new-habit

Cherry, K. The Yerkes-Dodson Law and Performance. verywellmind. Retrieved from https://www.verywellmind.com/what-is-the-yerkes-dodson-law-2796027

Craig, Torpy, Brennan & Burchett. (2010, July). The positive effects of office plants. Technical Nursery Papers, Issue no. 6. Retrieved from https://www.greenlifeindustry.com.au/Attachment?Action=Download&Attachment_id=1430

Craig, N. and Snook, S. (2014, May 1). From Purpose to Impact. Harvard Business Review.
Economy, P. (2018, February 28). This Is the Way You Need to Write Down Your Goals for Faster Success. Inc. Retrieved from https://www.inc.com/peter-economy/this-is-way-you-need-to-write-down-your-goals-for-faster-success.html

DeMers, J. (2017, June 22). 4 Surprising Ways Your Diet Is Affecting Your Productivity. NBC News. Retrieved from https://www.nbcnews.com/better/business/4-surprising-ways-your-diet-affecting-your-productivity-ncna775496

Dickinson, D. (2017, March 14). The link between nutrition and productivity in the workplace. LinkedIn. Retrieved from https://www.linkedin.com/pulse/link-between-nutrition-productivity-workplace-dave-dickinson/

Digdon, N. and Koble, A. (2011, May 24). Effects of Constructive Worry, Imagery Distraction, and Gratitude Interventions on Sleep Quality: A Pilot Trial. Applied Psychology: Health and Well Being Volume 3, Issue 2.

Drannan, J. (2016). The Relationship Between Physical Exercise and Job Performance: The Mediating Effects of Subjective Health and Good Mood. Arabian Journal of Business and Management Review. Retrieved from https://www.hilarispublisher.com/open-access/the-relationship-between-physical-exercise-and-job-performance-themediating-effects-of-subjective-health-and-good-mood-2223-5833-1000269.pdf

Feeling distracted? Here are 30 ideas to build your focus. (2019, May 23). Workminus.com. Retrieved from https://workminus.com/articles/workplace-distractions/

Foodtolive Team. (2017, January 5). Nutrition and Productivity: How Foods Can Affect Your Performance. HealthyBlog. Retrieved from https://foodtolive.com/healthy-blog/nutrition-productivity-foods-can-affect-performance/

Gino, F. (2016, April 14). Are You Too Stressed to Be Productive? Or Not Stressed Enough? Harvard Business Review. Retrieved from https://hbr.org/2016/04/are-you-too-stressed-to-be-productive-or-not-stressed-enough

Giving thanks can make you happier. (n.d.). Harvard Health Publishing. Retrieved from https://www.health.harvard.edu/healthbeat/giving-thanks-can-make-you-happier

Goyal, Singh, Sibinga, Gould, Rowland-Seymour, Sharma, Berger, Sleicher, Maron, Shihab, Ranasinghe, Linn, Saha, Bass, and Haythornthwaite. (2014, March). Meditation Programs for Psychological Stress and Well-Being: A Systematic Review and Meta-Analysis. Jama Intern Med.

Hamrick, K. (2016, November 7). Americans Spend an Average of 37 Minutes a Day Preparing and Serving Food and Cleaning Up. United States Department of Agriculture. Retrieved from https://www.ers.usda.gov/amber-waves/2016/november/americans-spend-an-average-of-37-minutes-a-day-preparing-and-serving-food-and-cleaning-up/

Helmer, J. (2019, January 13). 4 Good Reasons to Stop Hitting the Snooze Button. MyFitnessPal. Retrieved from https://blog.myfitnesspal.com/4-good-reasons-to-stop-hitting-the-snooze-button/?bb=disable

Hertz, R. (2002, November 11). Do scents affect people's moods or work performance? Scientific American. Retrieved from https://www.scientificamerican.com/article/do-scents-affect-peoples/

Hill, J. (2017, February 7). Why Having Indoor Plants Can Be Good For Your Business. Huffington Post. Retrieved from https://www.huffingtonpost.com.au/2017/06/28/why-having-indoor-plants-can-be-good-for-your-business_a_23007387/

Hindy, J. (n.d.). The Science Of Sleep: 8 Secrets About Sleep And Productivity I Wish I Knew Earlier. Lifehack. Retrieved from

https://www.lifehack.org/articles/productivity/the-science-of-
sleep-8-secrets-about-sleep-and-productivity-i-wish-i-knew-
earlier.html

How Luxembourg Rose To Becoming The World's Most
Productive Country? (2017). Retrieved from
https://steemit.com/luxembourg/@surpassinggoogle/how-
luxembourg-rose-to-becoming-the-world-s-most-productive-
country

How to Increase Your Productivity by 21% with Exercise. (n.d.).
Productivityist. Retrieved from
https://productivityist.com/increase-productivity-21-exercise/

Hulshof, B. (2013, May 31). The influence of colour and scent on
people's mood and cognitive performance in meeting rooms.
University of Twente. Retrieved from
https://essay.utwente.nl/63446/1/Hulshof_Bart_-
s_1128353_scriptie.pdf

Hyatt, M. (2016, February 17). 5 Reasons Why You Should Take a
Nap Every Day. Michael Hyatt & Co. Retrieved from
https://michaelhyatt.com/why-you-should-take-a-nap-every-
day/

Jäger, C. (2019, September 19). Take More Midday Naps. Life
Hacker. Retrieved from
https://www.lifehacker.com.au/2016/05/the-scientific-
benefits-of-midday-napping-explained-infographic/

Kennedy, M. (2015, December 25). How Do Successful People's
Sleep Patterns Compare To The Average American? Retrieved from
https://www.npr.org/sections/thetwo-
way/2015/12/24/460929475/how-do-successful-peoples-
sleep-patterns-compare-to-the-average-american

Lohr, V. (2010). Why Are the Benefits of Plants Indoors and Why Do We Respond Positively To Them? Acta Horticulturae, Department of Horticulture and Landscape Architecture, Washington State University. Retrieved from https://public.wsu.edu/~lohr/pub/2010LohrBenefitsPltsIndoors.pdf

McCarthy, N. (2019, February 5). Where Labor Productivity is Highest. Forbes. Retrieved from https://www.forbes.com/sites/niallmccarthy/2019/02/05/where-labor-productivity-is-highest-infographic/#233f8d14ea44

McKeown, G. (2014, April 15). Essentialism. Random House LLC.

Metev, D. (2019, September 3). How Much Time Do People Spend on Social Media? [63+ Facts to Like, Share and Comment]. Review 42. Retrieved from https://review42.com/how-much-time-do-people-spend-on-social-media/

Montini, L. (2014, June 13). What Unproductive Meetings Are Costing You (Infographic). Inc. Retrieved from https://www.inc.com/laura-montini/infographic/the-ugly-truth-about-meetings.html

Moody, G. (n.d.). The introduction of scents to an office area can increase productivity. Retrieved from https://fmlink.com/articles/the-introduction-of-scents-to-an-office-area-can-increase-productivity/

Mørch, A. (2017, August 31). A one hour meeting is never just a one hour meeting. AskCody. Retrieved from https://www.askcody.com/blog/infographic-a-one-hour-meeting-is-never-just-a-one-hour-meeting

Morin, A. (2015, April 3). 7 Scientifically Proven Benefits of Gratitude. Psychology Today. Retrieved from https://www.psychologytoday.com/us/blog/what-mentally-strong-people-dont-do/201504/7-scientifically-proven-benefits-gratitude

M. Moss, Hewitt, L. Moss, & Wesnes. (2008, January). Modulation of Cognitive Performance and Mood by Aromas of Peppermint and Ylang-Ylang. PubMed.

Mrazek, Franklin, Phillips, Baird, & Schooler. (2013, May). Mindfulness Training Improves Working Memory Capacity and GRE Performance While Reducing Mind Wandering. Psychol Sci.

Nutrition and Productivity: How Foods Can Affect Your Performance. (2017, January 5). HealthyBlog. Retrieved from https://foodtolive.com/healthy-blog/nutrition-productivity-foods-can-affect-performance/

Pozen, R. (2012, October 24). Exercise Increases Productivity. Brookings.   Retrieved   from https://www.brookings.edu/opinions/exercise-increases-productivity/

Productivity and sleep. (2020, May 5). Tuck. Retrieved from https://www.tuck.com/productivity-and-sleep/

Rampton, J. (2014, August 28). How Fortune 500 Leaders Spend Every Minute of the Day. Entrepreneur. Retrieved from https://www.entrepreneur.com/article/236853

Reed, D. (2016). How to Stop Getting Distracted and Get Work Done! Concierge Office Suites. Retrieved from https://theconciergeofficesuites.com/how-to-stop-getting-distracted-get-work-done/

The Right Outlook: How Finding Your Purpose Can Improve Your Life.   (n.d.).   Blue   Zones.   Retrieved   from https://www.bluezones.com/2011/08/the-right-outlook-how-finding-your-purpose-can-improve-your-life/

Romero, M. (2012, May 10). How Much Do Americans Really Exercise? Washingtonian. Retrieved from https://www.washingtonian.com/2012/05/10/how-much-do-americans-really-exercise/

Santos, G. (2018, March 15). 33 Ways to Increase Dopamine to Boost Your Productivity. Endless. Retrieved from https://helloendless.com/10-ways-to-increase-dopamine-to-boost-your-productivity/

Sharifzadeh, M. (2013). Does Fitness and Exercises Increase Productivity? Assessing Health,
Fitness and Productivity Relationship. California State Polytechnic University Pomona, American Journal of Management vol. 13(1). Retrieved from http://www.na-businesspress.com/AJM/SharifzadehM_Web13_1_.pdf

Sinek, S. (2010, May 4). How great leaders inspire action. YouTube. Retrieved from https://www.youtube.com/watch?v=qp0HIF3SfI4

Sleep, Performance, and Public Safety. (2007, December 18). Harvard Medical School, Division of Sleep Medicine. Retrieved from http://healthysleep.med.harvard.edu/healthy/matters/consequences/sleep-performance-and-public-safety

Staff Writer. (2019, March 20). Singapore ranked 2nd-happiest Asian nation in World Happiness Report. Yahoo News. Retrieved from https://sg.news.yahoo.com/singapore-ranked-2nd-happiest-asian-nation-world-happiness-report-023124001.html

Subbulaxmi & Programmer. (n.d.). Productivity and Stress. Retrieved from http://v2020eresource.org/content/files/stress_jul-sep02.pdf

Tate, C. (2015, July 12). 6 reasons why exercise can supercharge your productivity. The Next Web. Retrieved from https://thenextweb.com/lifehacks/2015/07/12/6-reasons-why-exercise-can-supercharge-your-productivity/

Warm & Parasuraman. (n.d.). Olfactory Stimulation and Sustained Attention. Retrieved from http://67-20-110-78.unifiedlayer.com/wp-content/uploads/2014/04/Olfactory_Stimulation_and_Sustained_Attention.pdf

What Scientific Studies Show Purpose Gives You. (n.d.). Retrieved from https://www.purposeguides.org/what-scientific-studies-show-purpose-gives-you#

What walking speeds say about us. (2007, May 2). Retrieved from http://news.bbc.co.uk/2/hi/uk_news/magazine/6614637.stm

What's in the Breakroom: Employee Diet and Productivity. (n.d.). 4imprint. Retrieved from https://info.4imprint.com/wp-content/uploads/1M-03-1009-Blue-Paper-A-Malnourished-Workforce.pdf

Widrich, L. (2014, February 2). What Happens To Our Brains When We Exercise And How It Makes Us Happier. Fast Company. Retrieved from https://www.fastcompany.com/3025957/what-happens-to-our-brains-when-we-exercise-and-how-it-makes-us-happier

About the Author

Michael Mehlberg is a husband, father, entrepreneur, business professional, author, fitness nut, organization freak, and productivity junkie. He helps high achievers consistently save time, get productive, and become more organized so they can live their passion and achieve their dreams. He currently lives in the greater Washington D.C. area with his wife and family.

Made in the USA
Las Vegas, NV
04 June 2021

24178778R00144